WHAT'S HAPPENING TO
THE AMERICAN FAMILY?

WHAT'S HAPPENING TO THE AMERICAN FAMILY?

SAR A. LEVITAN
and RICHARD S. BELOUS

THE JOHNS HOPKINS UNIVERSITY PRESS
Baltimore and London

This study was prepared under a grant from the Ford Foundation.

The Johns Hopkins University Press, Baltimore, Maryland 21218
The Johns Hopkins Press Ltd., London

Graphics by Al Lediard, Bailey Montague and Associates.

Library of Congress Cataloging in Publication Data

Levitan, Sar A.
  What's Happening to the American Family?

  Includes index.
    1. Family—United States.   2. Family policy—
  United States.   3. Social change.   I. Belous,
  Richard S.   II. Title.
  HQ536.L48   306.8'0973   81–47592
  ISBN 0–8018–2690–X   AACR2
  ISBN 0–8018–2691–8 (pbk.)

CONTENTS

PREFACE

American families seem to be besieged from all sides. Divorce rates are climbing; marriage is being postponed, if not rejected; fertility rates are falling; increasing numbers of children are being raised only by their mothers, either because of divorce or because their parents were never married; and housewives in record numbers are rushing out of the home and into the labor market. The predominance of the traditional household (a husband, wife, and children) is being challenged.

Constraints on personal behavior are also diminishing. Religious authority seems to be losing its hold, and sexual norms are changing radically and rapidly. The "Moral Majority" may have been successful at the ballot box but not in altering behavior. These basic changes are having a more profound impact on society than a whole host of social programs or technological innovations. They are neither abstract nor far away since millions of adults and children are affected by these shifts on a deeply personal level.

Freud called families the "germ cells" of civilization, and many social critics and the media have warned that a virulent disease is spreading. If the family cannot function, then who will raise and socialize the next generation? Even though society has created a vast array of institutions to provide many of the services and goods that were once the sole province of families, there are real constraints on what a welfare state can accomplish. These institutions outside of the home often have proven to be poor surrogate parents. Schools may teach most of the young reading, writing, and arithmetic, but many lessons are best learned within the home. The "bottom line" is a fear that if the family is unstable, then these pathologies are bound to have a pervasive deleterious impact not only on the quality of life but on the vitality of the body politic as well.

All these predictions about the disintegration of the family have some basis in fact. However, this book is not intended as an obituary of American families. Before we mourn for the family, it would be wise to look beyond a few simple statistics. American families are changing, but they are not eroding. The shifts in household structure are of two basic types. First, in the not too distant past there was one predominant household type, which consisted of a husband in the work force, a full-time housewife, and several children. The net result of recent events has been to make American family structure highly pluralistic—a phenomenon that is likely to last into the foreseeable future. A second factor has been at work even within more traditional husband-wife families. A majority of wives have entered the labor force. This shift has numerous implications that can jolt some families almost as much as a divorce. With wives contributing part of the family income, many women demand not only a more equal division of household chores but also a partnership in family decisionmaking.

The most worrisome data relating to the structure and stability of families are, of course, divorce rates. However, it is not at all clear that the divorce rate will continue to rise at the rapid pace chalked up during the 1960s and 1970s. There is no evidence that divorce rates will follow the results of the last election, but careful researchers may want to crank in the new conservative bend—among other variables—in their equations for projecting divorce rates.

As a result of these changes in both family structure and work roles, a growing number of children are being raised in single-parent families, and the number of female-headed households has climbed. Children raised by only their mothers face a significant increase in the chances that they will grow up in destitution.

The loosened knot and diversified American family structure has given rise to new concerns and anxieties. Whether or not society is better off because of the new sexual and household freedoms depends, in large measure, on personal value judgments. However, the ability to turn the clock back to an older, dominant family structure does not appear to be in the offing.

What are the solutions to these problems, assuming that there must be a solution to every problem? Much can be done to improve family life, including efforts by the federal government. A strict laissez-faire policy would be no better for families than it would be for the economy. Yet, in the American pluralistic society it is often futile even to spell out the general objectives that a family policy should take, as the 1980 White House Family Conference found out. Americans continue to resist having their family life fitted to any procrustean bed, and many seem to prefer more than one bed.

It should not be surprising that the problems engulfing an institution as pervasive as the family are receiving increasing public attention. A recent study found that 17 different federal government agencies administered 270 different family programs. The fact that there are so many programs should not be at all surprising because efforts in and out of the family involve income support, family planning, prenatal care of mothers, child care, education, school lunches, helping battered wives and abused children, and practically all human needs.

To sum up, the family should not be placed on the endangered species list. What we are seeing is a process of evolution. Government policies can ease the transition, but it will not be possible to turn the clock back to an earlier era of family structure. American households will remain highly pluralistic, and we must realize that along with the emerging new family structures and sexual freedoms will be a new list of discontents.

The tension stems from the desire to provide a stable family structure for the rearing of children and the continuation of society while at the same time attempting to achieve acceptable, and, one hopes, also satisfying and content lives. Many see no conflict between these two goals, yet a growing number can envision no simple or easy solution to what they regard as irremedial problems.

We are indebted to Mary Bedell, consulting editor; Alfred J. Kahn and Sheila B. Kamerman, both of Columbia University; S. M. Miller, Boston University; Martin Rein, M.I.T.; Marc Rosenbloom, Civil Rights Commission; Theodora Ooms, George Washington University; and Robert Taggart, Center for Employment Policy Studies, for their helpful critical comments. We are also grateful to Nancy Kiefer and Cathy Glasgow for shepherding the manuscript through several versions, and Al Lediard, Bailey Montague and Associates, for enlivening the prose with his illustrations.

This study was prepared under a grant from the Ford Foundation to the George Washington University's Center for Social Policy Studies. In accordance with the Foundation's practice, responsibility for the content was left completely to the authors.

Part One

FAMILY ALBUMS

Chapter One

SETTING THE STAGE

> Torvald: What a horrible awakening! All these eight
> years—she who was my joy and pride—a hypocrite. . . .
> Before all else, you are a wife and a mother.
> Nora: I don't believe that any longer. I believe before
> all else I am a reasonable human being just as you are.
> . . . I must think over things for myself and get to
> understand them. . . . I am going away from here. . . .
> Goodby, Torvald.
>
> Ibsen, *A Doll's House*

HARD TIMES

It was bad enough when Ibsen exposed theatergoers
to the world of syphilis and drugs, but having Nora walk out on her
husband was even more shocking to Victorian society. True, other
writers had confronted society with marriage without love, or even
love without marriage. An artist could depict a profligate Don Giov-
anni, just as long as the libertine was dragged down to hell in the
last act. An Anna Karenina or a Madame Bovary might seek sexual
bliss outside of the home, but they always seemed to meet the same
tragic fate by the end of the story.

Yet here was Ibsen showing the world a woman leaving her husband—not because he was an adulterer, a wife beater, a drunkard,
a financial wreck, or even impotent. Nora was leaving because her
marriage and family life lacked an almost ineffable quality. Far from
plunging his heroine into some inferno, the playwright held out a
new hope and vision for Nora. She had a chance—the first real
chance in her entire life—to find her identity and achieve self-

3

actualization or wholeness. No longer would she define herself as the "good" daughter, wife, or mother. To the contrary, a domestic hell was what she was leaving behind. No wonder Ibsen's play was a highly traumatic experience for many viewers.

But times, tastes, and mores have undergone dramatic changes since Ibsen's day. Today, such subject matter is deemed fit for broadcast even during the "prime time" family television hours. Far from being a rare tragedy, divorce, more often than not, is seen as ripe material for a TV situation comedy. Ibsen's subject matter has been repeated almost ad nauseam. The silver screen and the tube constantly bombard us with intimate scenes from a marriage headed for the rocks. Unmarried women seek new meaning in their lives; divorced men take a stab at starting over; and a world of Woody Allen characters find it impossible to determine who will be their lovers four weeks from now. Charlie Chaplin's revolving door sketch still has the power to bring us to laughter and tears, but now it is played with different lovers waiting on either side of the doorpost.

On the Rocks?

Marriage and family appear to have fallen on hard times. In a period of apparent breakdown of major social institutions, most observers greet the assumed demise of the family with alarm, but some radical thinkers welcome it. This sense of something falling apart has even reached the White House—a place normally noted for its pronouncements on enduring American virtues and piety. Both Democratic and Republican presidents have foreseen disturbing omens in current family trends. The Carter administration launched a nationwide White House Conference on Families in an effort to cope with these problems. Not to be outdone, Ronald Reagan proclaimed, upon accepting the Republican nomination, that his administration would be a crusade to revitalize American institutions. The first institution on his list was the family.

Assuming that where there's smoke, there's fire, the soothsayers cite evidence for their pessimistic view of the family's future. They call attention to the "critical" or "skyrocketing" divorce rates; fewer married couples are willing to remain married "until death do us part." Backing up the divorce statistics are powerful anecdotal stories. With divorce much more common, numerous individuals have witnessed the separation experience, either firsthand or through a relative or friend. Their reports of recrimination, anger, and often guilt, mixed with wrangling over child custody issues and messy property settlements, are enough to leave a sharp impression even on stoics. When the divorce involves children, the separation many times is a lingering crisis instead of a one-shot ordeal.

Besides divorce statistics and anecdotal tales, other evidence presumably pointing to a family malaise includes demographic statistics and data on female labor force participation rates. Contrary to the projected population explosion predicted by demographers a mere generation ago, the U.S. fertility rate recently has fallen to a historic nadir. Meanwhile, women in increasing numbers are not staying home to raise a smaller number of children and maintain a clean house; rather, they are seeking paid employment outside the home. The decline in the number of children, coupled with more time spent by women outside the house, are often cited as further proof that the family is withering.

Furthermore, shifts in sexual mores, social attitudes, religious beliefs, and laws affecting marriage and divorce are also buffeting the family. Beyond these forces, the expanding welfare state has encroached on many traditional services once exclusively provided by the family. This trend started with compulsory education; schools not only have replaced the family as the prime source of formal education for the young, but they also have become custodians of the children while both parents are at work. When hard times hit, people now have other sources to turn to for aid besides kith and kin. Social security makes provisions for orphaned children, and it also has sharply reduced the need for the elderly to depend on their children for financial support. Some analysts have pointed to specific government income support programs as one factor behind higher divorce rates and the growing number of unmarried couples. The grip of the family on the individual's life has been relaxed and its economic justification has been radically altered.

Added to all this is a highly mobile society in which the young are less inclined to follow in their parents' footsteps regarding how to live, where to live, what occupation to pursue, or even what to think and believe. Traditionally, a family has been an organization from which a person is hardly ever blackballed, and a home has been a place where a person is not refused shelter and food. But recently there has been less need to avail oneself of these family resources, and a growing number of individuals are finding alternatives to these traditional havens from a heartless world.

Nagging Fears

While some view the changing role of the family as an inevitable development of the affluent welfare state, others see it as another nail in the coffin of all the virtues and values that are being buried by modern society. For some—repeating an age-old lament—the weakening, if not the dissolution, of the family suggests that we are repeating the fatal mistakes of former great civilizations. Ancient Rome is said to have become decadent as the traditional family systems fell apart and individuals sought sexual gratifications where they could find them. One historian reports that the Roman Empire's civilization disintegrated when "the privileged classes ... came to find their ideals in pleasure. ... Men grew selfish and fixed their hearts on idleness and amusements."[1] Public morality became bastardized and was replaced by pursuit of pleasure sanctioned by Roman law and blessed by Roman gods. Giving such free reign to basic instincts that had been sublimated into producing a great culture, economy, and military force produced devastating results.

The nagging fears of repeating history are pervasive and shared by analysts representing widely divergent points on the political spectrum—and not just conservatives. For example, Robert L. Heilbroner, a left-of-center analyst, in sensing "the invisible approach of a distant storm," places domestic fears ahead of even war and the state of the economy as a prime source of our current anguish. He points to "the failure of the present middle-aged generation to pass its values along to its children" and views "extreme sexual relaxation" as adding to the disquieting "mood of our times."[2]

At the heart of the matter are deep forebodings about the future. If the family is not a viable institution, then what will sustain society? Who will raise the next generation and socialize it? How will basic values and norms be passed down and inculcated in children? Whether the concerns are justified or not, they exist. A decreased commitment to preserve a marriage through a lifetime, the worriers argue, is bound to affect the quality of life much more profoundly than a whole host of political, social, and technological changes.

The hypothesis is that the children of broken homes may undermine the stability of a society that condones such developments. Invoking Freud, Piaget, or Skinner, who, despite conflicting theories of personality development, agree that parents play a decisive role, supporters of the foregoing hypothesis argue that increasing numbers of unstable individuals denied a stable home life will rack society. Instead of Marx's industrial reserve army of unemployed, society will face a different sort of erosive reserve army. Depriving children during their crucial formative years of love, guidance, and role models provided by natural parents will not only thwart their development but will also have dire consequences for society. The products of broken homes will carry their scars first to the school system and then on to other social institutions. It will be difficult, if not impossible, for educators, social workers, police, the judicial system, and even employers to cope with this situation. Proxy institutions will not be able to provide the care or make up the deficiencies since they are, at best, poor substitutes for the family. A troubled family background augurs trouble when these children marry and form families of their own. At the root of this anxiety is the belief that if the family is headed for disruption, society as we know it cannot resist a similar fate.

At the other extreme is a vocal group that welcomes the dissolution of the family as a blessing that will free society from age-old shackles. They say amen to Bertrand Russell's assertion, "In its fullest development, [the family] was never very suitable either to urban populations or to seafaring people."[3] According to this hypothesis, the family is merely a part of the superstructure supporting bourgeois industrial society. Women are exploited in the home as in factories; in fact, women have recognized "the essential fact of housework right from the very beginning; which is that it stinks."[4]

The bourgeois family, according to the pronouncements of the institution's detractors, is neither the only structure nor necessarily the best or most efficient one that the human mind could create to produce true social harmony. For many individuals, it is argued, the traditional family experience leaves a sense of alienation just as strong and scars just as deep as a broken home. The vast increase in the divorce rate testifies to the increasing obsolescence of the old way and manifests its fragility in modern society. All the efforts to preserve the institution cannot hide the inherent discontent that it breeds. Men and women in Henry David Thoreau's state of quiet desperation are, at long last, being liberated. Increasingly, they do not feel chained down for life. Many of our grandparents and parents, if they had had our new-found freedoms and opportunities, would have used them to better their situation. Indeed a broken home may provide a far healthier environment for a child than one where the parents are engaged in incessant warfare.

But change, no matter how necessary, does not come easily, and those who choose to throw off family shackles are subject, in the words of Eric Hoffer, to a wrenching "ordeal of change." As we enter the uncharted waters of what some analysts call a postindustrial society, fundamental institutions inevitably will change, and some will be swept away. Long ago DeTocqueville observed: "What we call necessary institutions are often no more than institutions to which we have grown accustomed." According to this argument, new alternatives are forming to replace the family and traditional marriage. The emerging economic order will require a vastly different superstructure. Some analysts envision a scenario where "paternal authority gives way to the collective authority . . . and postindustrial leisure society then appears to offer, according to age or taste, multiple channels of socialization which used to be the prerogative of the family unit. . . . "[5]

Statistics show that the so-called "normal" family—a working husband, a full-time housewife, and two or more children—now represents only a fraction of U.S. families. For example, at the close of the 1970s, divorced, separated, widowed, and never-married women headed more than 8 million families, or one of every seven in the United States. About 10 to 15 percent of couples never have children, while about 5 percent of the American population will never marry, and about 7 percent live alone. Thus, the living arrangements of more than 75 percent of the population differ from the so-called "normal" family, and these arrangements should be viewed as just as legitimate as the traditional household model.

The Economist's Perspective

It may come as a surprise that economists—who often have shed more confusion than light on matters in their own sphere—should venture onto a turf well trod by practitioners of other disciplines, including anthropology, sociology, and psychology. Ironically, the institution of the family and related problems were the first issues tackled by ancient economic thinkers. In fact, the word economics is derived from the Greek word *oikonomia*, which means household management.

Recently, economists have expanded their traditional turf by attempting to illuminate decisionmaking processes for allocating resources not only in the marketplace but also in other human endeavors. Racial discrimination, fertility, politics, crime, education, statistical decisionmaking, uses of leisure time, and even marriage decisions in a sense all deal with choices concerning the allocation of scarce resources. As one noted economist put it, "Economic theory may well be on its way to providing a unified framework for all behavior involving scarce resources, nonmarket as well as market, nonmonetary as well as monetary, small group as well as competitive."[6]

He is not the first, nor is he likely to be the last, to place high hopes on the future of his discipline, even though the profession's recent record does not hold much promise for such euphoria. Whatever economic theory can contribute to the study of the family, it is clear that the family's evolution will profoundly influence the future of the economy. Many economic, political, and social issues are tied up with the family. The household is the prime unit of consumption. The composition of the family will largely determine the types and quantity of goods and services demanded from the American economy. Family decisions influence the number and types of workers seeking employment, and economic models that do not consider family-related variables tend to do a poor job in predicting labor force participation rates.

In our welfare state, massive government transfer payments, or income support, provide roughly one of every six dollars of disposable personal income, and about one-third of the population receives these payments. The system of income support required to meet basic needs depends largely on the condition and role of the family. So does the prescription for welfare reform. Without exaggeration, the type of society and economy we shall have in many ways hinges on the conditions and fate of the family.

A RESILIENT INSTITUTION

A straight-line extrapolation could predict a bleak future for the family. The birth rate has fallen to a very low level and may remain so as more people choose to raise one or no children. With more options, fewer people may count marriage and families as necessary ingredients of the good life.

At the same time, the straight-line prognosticators predict that continuation of the recent divorce rate will produce a relative and absolute increase in the number of broken homes. More children will live in homes lacking one or both parents and more women will enter the labor force and give up on families.

Still Strong

Many of these conclusions are seriously flawed because they are based on cursory and selective data. Human behavior *is* subject to change, and human decisions rarely follow straight-line extrapolations. Numerous reasons back up the striking conclusion that marriage and the family are not headed for the rocks. Careful analysis shows some very real and wrenching changes, but also some strong indications that the family is a far more resilient social institution than is often supposed. It is, as Margaret Mead noted, "the toughest institution we have."[7]

Several key variables affecting family life, including fertility and marriage rates, suggest that current trends will *not* continue. Social and economic forces may actually buttress the family institution, even though it continues to evolve. The increased participation of women in the labor force may either delay marriage, contribute to its dissolution, or reduce birth rates, but other developments will not necessarily weaken the family and certainly not increase the rejection of marriage and motherhood. In fact, a multiple–pay check household *can* lead to a far stronger and more stable family. As more women combine careers with motherhood, their labor force participation rate could change the usually assumed outcome. With its heightened reliance on part-time employment, a service economy could be more amenable to the dual aspirations of women.[8] And advances in birth control, enabling better spacing of children, allow women to combine motherhood with careers, although achieving both requires struggle and sacrifice.

A closer look at the major variables affecting the family may be painful to Victorians, but it does not depict a rejection or even the long-run demise of the institution of marriage and family. The family has changed its nature, but it shows every indication of remaining a central social and economic fact of life. Few other institutions have shown as much diversity, resiliency, and ability to adapt and evolve over time as the relationships among kin.

fam·i·ly (fam/ə lē, fam/lē), *n.*, *pl.* **-lies,** *adj.* **—***n.* **1.** parents and their children, whether dwelling together or not. **2.** the children of one person or one couple collectively: *My wife and I want a large family.* **3.** the spouse and children of one person: *I'm taking my family on vacation next week.* **4.** any group of persons closely related by blood, as parents, children, uncles, aunts, and cousins: *She married into a socially prominent family.* **5.** all those persons considered as descendants of a common progenitor: *The Tudor family reigned long.* **6.** *Chiefly Brit.* approved lineage, esp. noble, titled, famous, or wealthy ancestry: *young men of family.* **7.** a group of persons who form a household under one head, including parents, children, servants, etc. **8.** the staff, or body of assistants, of an official: *the office family.* **9.** a group of related things or people: *the family of romantic poets; the halogen family of elements.*

The Random House Dictionary of the English Language, The Unabridged Edition. Copyright © 1981 . . . 1966 by Random House, Inc.

The *family* has meant many different things to different societies. Polygamous and extended families at one time were, of course, the social norm. Some analysts propose that the current family is obsolete, and it will be replaced by communal living arrangements. The federal department most closely associated with the family recently defined the institution to include any "group of persons who share physical and emotional resources over a long period of time, and whose adult members have, had or will have, as one central purpose the rearing of children."[9] Webster's dictionary defines a family as a "group of persons of common ancestry . . . living under one roof." While the concept is sufficiently flexible to conform to personal tastes, the term connotes a deep and sustained commitment, usually in the form of marriage. In the Western world during the last few centuries, common usage has implied two adults of opposite sexes who are living together with their offspring and other blood or adopted relatives and whose relationship has been sanctioned by either the state, the established religious authorities, or both. This contract carries with it the presumption of responsibility for the offspring of the union.

Many would argue that this definition of a family excludes more than 1 million unmarried couples who reported to government enumerators that they are keeping house together. The arbitrary definition used here is not designed to convey any normative value judgments, but to avoid the fallacy of circular reasoning. If a family is defined to include any possible system of relationships, then, of course, the family is here to stay—short of a nuclear holocaust. The analysis of today's family and its future can take on any real meaning only when the notion of the family is given specific form.

Evolution, Not Dissolution

The bulk of the ruminations on the current status and future of the family have tended to be either alarmist or utopian. In either case, it is assumed that the family is in an almost hopeless state of disintegration. The alarmists issue dire warnings; the utopians respond with shouts of joy. It is more reasonable to interpret the strains and changes being experienced within American family life as signs of evolution. Public policy can help to channel this process in a constructive direction, but it cannot turn back the clock.

The rest of this study backs up this conclusion in detail, explores its policy implications, and argues that the paradigm of evolution sheds more light on family issues than analyses based on the assumption of dissolution.

If the hypothesis concerning the demise or obsolescence of the family is correct, then one would expect to see a dramatic shift in certain basic values. However, as has been demonstrated in numerous attitudinal survey research projects, family life and marriage are still widely considered critical to many aspects of personal stability and development. The shift in basic values has not been as widespread as anecdotal stories or reports in the media would seem to indicate.

Survey research finds no major significant statistical difference among various adult age groups concerning marital satisfaction. Even young adults still indicate that family life and marriage are two of the most important factors contributing to a "normal" and "productive" life. As a leading public opinion surveyor put it, "Any belief that Americans do not place top priority on the family and family life is completely refuted."[10] The preponderance of adult Americans continue to marry, and despite a major increase in the divorce rate, over 80 percent of husbands and wives are still in their first marriage. Given current trends, this percentage will fall, but will remain well above a majority.

Prior to 1940 the annual divorce rate in America was about 2 per 1,000. It rose after World War II, headed down during the 1950s, and then rose to 5.2 per 1,000 by 1979. If the current level of divorce continues, the proportion of marriages ending in divorce may hit as high as 2 per 5. In 1979 there was one divorce for every two marriages. Projections indicate that about 38 percent of first marriages by women between the ages of 25 and 29 will end in divorce, but three of every four divorcees will remarry, and 45 percent of those who remarry will go through divorce once again.[11] There are indications that the divorce rate may be stabilizing at close to the current levels, and some demographers even anticipate a slow reversal of the trend. The divorce rates may not fall to the low levels of pre-1940, but neither do they seem to be progressing geometrically, as it is often assumed.

Averages covering all age groups sometimes hide more information than they reveal, but not in this case. Perhaps the data suggest a stabilization because they include the status of older, and presumably more traditional, couples. However, disaggregation of divorce data by age does not support this hypothesis. The divorce rate for persons between the ages of 30 and 44 years was almost 19 percent higher than that for those under 30 at the end of the 1970s. Couples under 30 are not uniquely unstable compared with other adult age groups when it comes to ending marriages. Even if divorce rates remain high compared with previous eras, it does not follow that they will vastly increase as the current generation of younger adults grows older.

Married couples have not rejected having children, although they do want fewer children. Many younger couples have postponed having children, but as in the past only a few wish to remain childless. This situation could contain many benefits for individual families and society; striving for quality instead of quantity would allow families to allocate greater per capita resources to fewer children. There are even indications that the fertility rate may increase somewhat from its current low level.

The number of children involved in a divorce has more than tripled since 1956. The number of families headed by a woman and the number of children living with only one parent also have increased. Yet almost seven of ten children live with their natural parents, and nearly all children live with at least one parent. One parent might not be as satisfactory an arrangement as two, but at least children today have a much higher chance of being with either a mother or father than those in previous generations, when adults were more likely to die or to be unable to support their children.

Estimates indicate that about 45 percent of the children born in the mid-1970s will live in a one-parent family at least some time before their 18th birthday. But high remarriage rates will make this a temporary experience in most cases. Only about one of ten children in a two-parent family is living with a stepparent.[12] The average number of children per divorce has decreased as the proportion of divorces involving no young children has increased. The notion, therefore, that a rapidly escalating number of children will be involved in divorce is not supported by recent data.

It is very important to look behind simple statistics. Fifty-two percent of the households headed by divorced or separated women contained no children at the end of the 1970s. With 22 percent of all marriages involving at least one divorced person, it appears that recent household shifts show a far more complex pattern than a simple rejection of the family. For many younger adults the first marriage without children appears to be almost a quasi tryout or preparatory period for the second marriage, which most often results in having children.

Women's increased participation in the work force hardly indicates their rejection of family life. While a woman's economic independence may lead to divorce, her "gainful" employment often keeps a family together. As more women enter the labor force, more

husbands and children will have to take on greater housework responsibilities, and the working women will probably demand a
greater say in how the family's money is spent. All this indicates
some basic shifts in stereotyped sex roles. But the institution of the
family has shown itself to be highly resilient and amenable to change.

Hurrah?

Suppose that the family is heading for evolution and
not dissolution; why sing hosanna? Despite all the family's visible
warts and blemishes, no society has yet created a better and more
enduring method of raising its young and passing on basic social
values. History is rife with attempts to form alternatives. The kibbutz
movement of Israel is frequently cited, but only 3 percent of the
Israelis live in kibbutzim. Communist governments, after first downgrading families, have more recently decreed "pro-family" policies.
In brief, alternative arrangements have failed to provide viable substitutes and realistic options to families that are acceptable to the
majority of the population.

While most American youngsters now learn to read, write, and
do arithmetic in schools outside the home, they still need to learn
much from their families. Constraints of cost effectiveness and resources limit the delegation of functions usually performed by the
family to alternative institutions. Our welfare state can handle cases
of dire emergency, but if these exceptions became the norm, we
would all be driven to the poor house.

Only rarely has our society removed children from their homes
and placed them in either public or private institutions. Instead, it
has chosen—through income transfers; in-kind subsidies, such as
food stamps and housing allowances; and other human resource
policies—to provide the wherewithal to bolster the family and help
it rear the young. It has been charged that these social welfare efforts
have sometimes split up families so that they may receive these
benefits. Recent proposals and reforms have tried to mitigate these
unwanted outcomes. Yet it would be rash to assume that the bulk
of public policy efforts have harmed family life. In many cases public
aid is required to maintain a family as a viable unit.

Prophets of the "Brave New World" may foresee, or even advocate, that alternative institutions should take over the functions of
the family, including even the biological functions of reproduction.
However, the creation of such a utopia, or dystopia, would require
a yearning to follow these options. More importantly, it would require a far more radical change in basic human desires. Most of us

need to achieve self-realization and to be creative members of society. But, as few of us have the ability to fulfill these desires as philosophers and poets, satisfying the need must take a far more mundane, but positive, form. Most of us need, to paraphrase Sigmund Freud, work and love, which can be achieved only by a sustained commitment instead of fly-by-night arrangements. Are marriage and children a necessary part of this commitment? Obviously not in all cases, but they are in the vast majority—whether now, in the past, or the future.

The popular bleak scenario for the family contains a good deal of social instability. Fortunately, a critical analysis of the evidence does not paint such a dire picture, and thus a heartfelt "hurrah" is in order. The family is much more than a fiction of bourgeois society or a product of the industrial revolution. Indeed, it may be as old as humanity itself; according to the Bible, once Adam established some order in his environment, God gave him woman from his loin. The study of our early ancestors shows that men and women have sought stable households since time immemorial. As Richard Leakey and Roger Lewin put it, families "are not just inventions of anthropologists anxious to analyze the lives of technologically primitive people by carving up their social structure into objective but somewhat artificial units."[13] Whether a tribe, an extended family, or a nuclear unit, these institutions have provided an important foundation for identity and a stable outlet for the expression of basic human needs.

Even with a historic perspective and an eye on the new order favored by some, recent shifts in American families demand that policymakers and the concerned public show greater interest in how other social institutions interact with families. For example, family background can have a major impact on the types of remedial employment, training, and welfare policies required and the outcomes of specific programs. Facing up to these interrelationships is difficult but necessary.

Recent survey research tends to back up the conclusion that families and parenthood are hardly out of fashion as far as young adults are concerned. This is true even for women who graduate from prestigious colleges and face the highest expected opportunity costs from motherhood.[14] Whether or not young adults are able to meet a majority of their family and career expectations remains to be seen. But there is every indication that a growing number of young adults are trying to achieve a workable compromise that includes both aspirations.

While the family is in a process of evolution, it should be recognized that the process is perpetual. One should not conclude that a hands-off laissez-faire policy offers the best alternative, because active human resource policies can improve conditions in many areas. As far as the family is concerned, we probably face a period in which we will muddle through and cope. But kinship has always dealt with these difficulties. It is far easier to paint gloomy pictures of doom and dissolution than to face up to existing circumstances. These are neither the worst of times nor the best of times for the family. Therein lie our challenges and opportunities.

Part Two

THE FAMILY IN ACTION:
THE KNOT LOOSENS

Chapter Two

LOVE AND MARRIAGE

"You don't think one needs the experience of having
been married?" she asked. "Do you think it need be an
experience?" replied Ursula. "Bound to be, in some
way or other," said Gudrun coolly. "Possibly
undesirable, but bound to be an experience of some
sort." "Not really," said Ursula. "More likely to be the
end of experience."

D. H. Lawrence, *Women in Love*

BASIC VALUES

It is often assumed that a growing number of people
echo and subscribe to Ursula's view of marriage. But in matters of
the heart, Lawrence knew and was able to capture the complex web
of often contradictory desires and values. The irony is that in the
end of the novel it is Ursula, more than any other of Lawrence's
characters, who seeks fulfillment through a stable marriage. She
might start off disdaining marriage, but—before the story is all told—
she is the one who rejects experimentation with new forms of sexual
and love relationships. "You are enough for me. I don't want any-
body else but you. Why isn't it the same with you?" she asks her
husband. When told of new forms of love to replace marriage, Ursula
views them as "an obstinacy, a theory, a perversity. . . . You can't
have it, because it's false, impossible."

Attitudinal Findings

A dramatic shift in basic family values has not taken
place, contrary to media reports. A far different picture emerges in
national attitudinal polls concerning marriage and the family. Ac-

cording to sociologist Amitai Etzioni, if the present rate of increase in divorce and single households continues to accelerate as it did in the late 1960s and 1970s, by mid-1990 "not one American family will be left."[1] While Etzioni indulges in hyperbole, the thrust of his prediction is that the forces that have buffeted the family will accelerate the erosion of the family beyond the damage done in the past two decades. However, statistical evidence and other indications back up the position that the divorce rate will not grow nearly as rapidly in the future and may even become stabilized.

National attitudinal surveys seem to support the above inference. A recent Louis Harris poll found that 85 percent of American men indicated that family life was very important for a happy and satisfied life. In contrast, less than half considered sex as very important for personal happiness, but married men reported higher levels of satisfaction with their sex lives than single men. When asked to list the factors that in their opinion contributed most to happiness, only health and love were ranked higher than family life. A Gallup survey backed up these findings, and data disaggregated by sex, race, education, geographic location, and age show that family life and marriage are still very highly rated. Adults in all subgroups emphasize family life as a means of finding personal fulfillment.[2]

Despite these statistical averages, dramatic shifts may still be taking place. The opinions and values of younger men might sharply diverge from older—and, in general, more conventional—people, so that future surveys might show an additive and accelerated pattern. However, survey research does not show a vast difference in basic values among generations. Roughly five of eight students believe that families are essential for a happy life, and this proportion increased during the 1970s.[3] Apparently, most of the young still consider family life critical to many aspects of personal happiness despite the vast social changes of recent years. In fact, attitudinal research into basic values shows that few social institutions have fared as well as the family during this stormy period.

Marriage

Marriage, in fact, is experienced by almost all Americans at some time. Some may delay it or terminate it, but very few do not try it. When it comes to marriage, women are apparently more precocious than men (figure 1). One-half of all men who marry enter their first marriage by age 24, and the same proportion of women do so two years earlier. Before they meet their Maker, 94 percent of men and 96 percent of women have said "I do" at least once.[4] This figure is slightly higher than that in the nineteenth century, which sometimes was only 90 percent.[5] During colonial times, the marriage rate might have been as low as 84 percent in certain areas.[6] Some analysts have predicted that the proportion of men and women who marry may drop a little below the current historically high levels. But it is highly unlikely that it will fall to the low rates reported during the early part of this century or during the 1800s.

While virtually all Americans take the marriage vows, recently they have been postponing this event. In 1960, only one of four men and one of ten women had never married by age 26. By the end of the 1970s, the comparable rates had increased to roughly three of ten men and more than one of five women. Yet, by the time men and women reached their 34th birthday, the rate of never-married people was virtually the same at the end of the 1970s as in 1960. For men and women aged 35 and over, the trend has been in the opposite direction, falling since 1960. Fewer people in their late teens or early 20s have married, but for more mature people the propensity toward marriage has not radically altered.

The postponement of marriage is not a new phenomenon but it represents a cyclical fluctuation. In 1890, the median age of the first

FIGURE 1.

Nineteen of 20 Americans marry before they reach middle age.

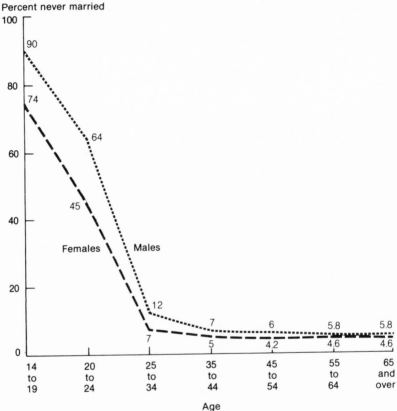

Source: U.S., Department of Commerce, Bureau of the Census

marriage for men was 26.1 years and 22 years for women, compared with age 22.8 for men and 20.3 for women in 1960. By 1977, the median age at the first marriage (24 years for men and 22 years for women) was almost the same as in 1940, just before the United States entered World War II.

The tendency to postpone saying the magical words "I do" need not necessarily dishearten even traditionalists. In fact, many positive social consequences could result from the trend to delay marriage. More young women have decided to continue their education and seek other experiences or even establish a career before marriage, rather than move from their parents' home directly into one where a husband and children wait in the wings. Also, during the Vietnam War a major proportion of young men postponed marriage while in the armed forces and others enrolled in universities to avoid military service. These activities did not preclude marriage but tended to reduce the chances of seeking wedding bells.

Complications arising from the post–World War II baby boom and recent economic conditions also have played a role in delaying marriage. Women reaching the usual ages when a majority of them first marry (that is, 18 to 24) experienced a "marriage squeeze." Women in this age group outnumbered men aged 20 to 26—the normal age when men first marry.[7] Also, the economy did not generate enough jobs for the products of the baby boom when they entered the labor market. Two economic recessions during the 1970s—including the deepest and most prolonged slump since World War II—made the going even harder for young workers than for the more mature. Given loose labor markets and the unprecedented number of youths reaching working age, many young people believed that they lacked adequate financial assets for starting a family. Recent bouts with inflation have not made their financial prospects any brighter.

Changes in attitudes toward sex outside of marriage also have had an impact on postponing marriage. Both the pronounced increase in premarital sexuality and the broader acceptance of this behavior have been thoroughly documented. The proportion of adults sanctioning premarital coitus rose from one-fifth in the early 1960s to more than one-half in the 1970s. Young adults have apparently been cooperative in acting out societal approval. According to recent surveys only about one of every four blushing brides was a virgin upon entering marriage. While premarital coitus has been high among lower-income and minority groups, a major factor behind this upward trend has been the increased sexual activity among young college-educated adults from families with relatively high incomes.[8]

The standard "Dutch uncle advice" to young men used to be not to rush into marriage: first, go out and live a bit, or even "sow your oats," and then ground yourself firmly before taking a wife and raising a family. The image created by Charles Dickens of poverty— a landlord beating at the door, a half-dozen crying, hungry, and sniffling children, an unhappy and nagging spouse, and poor prospects for economic advancement—was enough to make a young man think twice before being tied down too early. In 1890, the median age for men to marry—a relatively ripe 26—was seen as a healthy sign for the future of family stability.

While few Dutch uncles are reported to have told their nieces to go out and sow their oats before marriage, there are reasons for believing that delaying marriage is a healthy sign. One of the best predictors of divorce and separation is the age of marriage. Marriages at a very young age have a far higher probability of ending in divorce than those at a more mature age.[9] The time spent during a person's early twenties picking up added doses of education and credentials, labor market experience, accumulating financial resources, and even sexual knowledge, can be used to build up a supply of "human capital"—to use the economist's terminology—that can be used to foster a stable and productive family life. The postponement of marriage, therefore, should not be viewed as either reflecting the downgrading of marriage or a temporary rejection of marriage.

A Marriage Calculus?

Marital patterns over the life cycle, including the timing and incidence of marriage and divorce, have changed, but most Americans still marry at least once. Focusing an economist's lens on marriage may prove fruitful in understanding its almost universal appeal. Using a technique that may seem arcane to some, but not surprising to others, economists have applied benefit-cost analysis to marriage. Marriage, one can assume, is a free exchange, which, like other commodity trading, increases the level of utility, or well-being, of marriage partners compared to single individuals. As men and women seek out mates, a marriage market is presumed to exist. Economists do not claim that two can always live as cheaply as one, but a family may achieve economies of scale in its human endeavors. The list of gains from marriage often includes improved quality and lower price for household-produced commodities such as health, food and shelter, recreation, sex, companionship, and even children.[10]

The era of building economic models to predict marriage conditions is still in its very early formative years, and skeptics may properly doubt whether the models will ever reach maturity. Even if the current state of the analysis is superficial and simplistic, the approach suggests that very powerful economic and social forces lie behind the continued pattern of marriage.

Some economists apply traditional international trade theory and comparative advantage to their analysis of marriage. Economists have long favored free trade among nations, arguing that all participants are winners. For example, if nation A produces wine more efficiently than textiles, and nation B produces textiles more efficiently than wine, then under a wide range of prices both nations will gain from international trade. By utilizing their respective comparative advantages, both nations can increase output and peoples' sense of welfare.

The economic gains from marriage are the sum of the value of household production and money income received from employment outside the household. To use a very simple example, suppose the value of household production and money income for two single people were:

	Value of household production	Money income	Value of total output
Male	$2,000	$10,000	$12,000
Female	2,000	6,000	8,000
		Total	$20,000

If these two individuals were married and concentrated their efforts on that production area where they showed a comparative advantage, then the value of production could be as follows:

	Value of household production	Money income	Value of total output
Male	0	$14,000	$14,000
Female	$8,000	0	8,000
		Total	$22,000

Based on this illustration, the overall economic gains produced by marriage are not apparent. All that the comparative advantage theory of marriage demonstrates is that two single people can often live better as one household. It does not require that the people be married. With the rapid growth in the number of unmarried couples in the United States, many individuals are finding it possible to enjoy the benefits of comparative advantage without the sanction of either church or state. As long as the model builders overlook such "details," they have a long way to go before they illuminate the institution of marriage.

Researchers who do not use econometric models also have reached a similar conclusion about the real gains from marriage. For example, sociologist Jessie Bernard has examined the scope of advantages, or benefits, accruing from marriage, and she has concluded that they are quite sizable—at least for males.[11] The physical health of married men in middle age tends to be better than that of single men. Also, the mental health of married men is superior to that of unmarried males, and marriage, she claims, is a clear and important positive variable in a man's career, including his earning power. Bernard cites data that indicate that the rate of mental depression is more than 35 percent higher for single than for married men. Median income is about 52 percent higher for married than for single men, while one of four married men is a professional or managerial worker, compared with only one of five single men.

It might be argued, however, that this type of analysis places the cart before the horse, and the results are not due to the beneficent effects of marriage itself. Instead, men who marry—and stay married—may be, on the average, healthier, more emotionally stable, and in occupations with higher earnings and status than single men. If this were the situation, then a stable marriage would be a result, and not a cause, of these statistical differences.

Bernard has tried to test the benefits of marriage by comparing married and unmarried men of the same general background. Her statistical tests indicate that a major portion of the reported psychological, social, health, and labor market differences appear to be caused by—or due to—marriage. When other variables are considered, it is marriage that seems to explain and predict those males who would experience such gains as higher earnings, more stable jobs, and better health. Further strong evidence that marriage produces major benefits for men is that, once they have tried it, they can hardly live without it. A vast majority of divorced and widowed men remarry, and roughly half of all divorced white men who remarry do so within three years after their divorce. "Indeed, it might not be far-fetched to conclude that the verbal assaults on marriage indulged in by men are a kind of compensatory reaction to their dependence on it," Bernard concludes.[12]

The psychological, social, health, and labor market benefits garnered by married women do not appear to be as strong as those secured by married men. For example, the rate of depression among married women is about 45 percent higher than the rate for married men, and slightly fewer wives than husbands report that their marriages are "very happy." Also, the labor market benefits of greater income and higher social status occupations are smaller for married women than for married men. Yet, despite the sex differential in benefits, married women often show statistically significant gains from marriage when compared with single women.

Social scientists are still a long way from producing statistical models, or a calculus of marriage, that can accurately explain and predict marriage decisions by men and women in the real world. Any predictions about the future of the family must, therefore, rely upon past and current data as well as some value judgments. An institution that persists despite vast social, political, and economic upheavals is not likely to be abandoned in the foreseeable future, although its role may continue to undergo changes.

UNTIL DEATH?

Granted that Americans have not given up on the institution of marriage, it does not follow that men and women are still willing to remain tied down with the same marriage partner until they meet their Maker. The much-publicized statistics do show a strong propensity by Americans to accept divorce and remarriage rather than one official partner for a lifetime. However, a critical scrutiny of divorce and remarriage data does not show a society that has replaced the family with a random, never-ending game of musical chairs (or beds). Instead, they indicate that while more people end their marriages in divorce, most of these individuals attempt quickly to form new stable relationships. Repeating the cycle of divorce and remarriage for a third time is confined to a relatively small portion of the population. Mickey Rooney and Zsa Zsa Gabor are not representative of the American family. Most people who remarry stick with the second partner and do not try again.

Divorce

The most worrisome data on the changing structure of the American family are, of course, the divorce rates. Until World War II, the United States had a relatively low rate of marriages ending in divorce (about 2 per 1,000 population). The war produced a boom crop of marriages followed by an increase in the relative number of divorces, a phenomenon that was repeated following the Vietnam War (figure 2). Apparently many of the wartime unions did not last, and by 1946 the divorce rate hit 4.3—an all-time high up to that point.

Within a few years, the "quickie" war marriages were dissolved and the divorce rate returned to its pre–World War II level. However, in the 1960s the divorce rate started upward in an almost inexorable—and possibly even alarming—climb. It hit 3.2 per 1,000 pop-

FIGURE 2.

Both the number of divorces and the divorce rate have climbed to new highs.

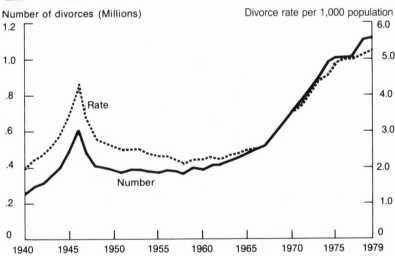

Source: U.S., Department of Commerce, Bureau of the Census

ulation by the end of the turbulent 1960s and continued to rise in the presumably conservative climate of the 1970s. By 1973 the divorce rate had surpassed the highs recorded following World War II, reaching 5.2 per 1,000 in 1979. If the recent trends continue on a lifetime basis, then the proportion of marriages ending in divorce could be close to 40 percent.[13] In 1979 there was one divorce for every two marriages.

Besides the number of divorces and the divorce rates, the ratios of ever-divorced persons to persons in intact marriages indicate that marriage dissolution has become a widespread phenomenon. Starting from a higher relative base than whites, the divorce rate for blacks has increased by 213 percent during the 1960–78 period, compared with an increase of 151 percent for whites:[14]

Divorce rates per 1,000 married
persons with spouse present

Year	Total	White	Black
1978	90	83	194
1970	47	44	83
1965	41	39	70
1960	35	33	62

The rise in divorce rates applied to all age groups but was highest for people under 30 followed by persons between the ages of 30 to 44. However, even for people 65 years and over the divorce rate increased by 84 percent:

Divorce rates per 1,000 married persons
with spouse present

Year	Under 30 years	30 to 44 years	45 to 64 years	65 years and over
1978	91	108	84	59
1970	38	47	53	47
1965	28	41	48	45
1960	23	33	46	32

Even these data on divorce rates, disturbing as they may be for the stability of the family, must be supplemented. An analysis of data on the growth of nontraditional family structures places the picture of the American household even more out of focus. From 1970 to 1979, the number of households headed by a female with no husband present increased by about 45 percent to more than 8 million. At the same time, the number of women heading a household because of a marital separation—instead of a divorce—rose by 54 percent to almost 1.5 million. The increase in marital separation—as an alternative or waiting period to divorce—was larger for white than minority women. In addition to rising separation and divorce rates, there has also been an increase in the number of unmarried couples living together and families headed by unmarried women.

On the other hand, while the divorce and separation data dramatically indicate that divorce and marital separation have become more a part of the American way of life, they may also exaggerate the impression that the disintegration of the family is at hand. It's a case of focusing on how much of the glass is empty and how much is full. Two of every three first marriages entered into today can be expected to last for a lifetime. At the same time, 40 percent of all marriages can be predicted to end in divorce, because about 44 percent of divorced individuals who remarry will be redivorced, thus pushing up the total projection for marriages that will end in divorce.

Also, marital disruption within American society has not grown as much as these divorce estimates suggest. Research by sociologist Mary Jo Bane indicates that marital disruption was also a problem in the "good old days," even though its causes have shifted. With vast improvements in health, plunging death rates for all ages counterbalanced increases in the divorce rate during this century to such a degree that the rate of marital disruption for all causes was fairly stable until 1970. Bane found that the percentage of "ever-married" women living with their first husbands had changed very little during the twentieth century:[15]

	Age of women		
Year	45–49 years	50–54 years	55–64 years
1910	70.2	64.7	55.0
1940	68.4	64.0	54.9
1970	69.9	65.7	56.6

The offset of the growing divorce rate by the falling death rate cannot, however, be expected to continue. Advancements in medical science probably cannot counteract a rapid and continued increase in the divorce rate. If this is the case, the overall incidence of marital disruption could surpass earlier experience.

It is not at all clear, however, that the divorce rate will continue to grow in the future as it did during the decade prior to 1975 (figure 3). In some years during the 1960s, the annual increase in the divorce rate exceeded 4 percent per year and the rate accelerated in the early 1970s. Between 1968 and 1975, the average annual increase was over 8 percent, compared with 2 percent during the succeeding four years. If this trend continues, the near future should not be as dis-

FIGURE 3.

The divorce rate appears to be stabilizing.

Percent change in the divorce rate from the previous year

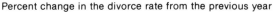

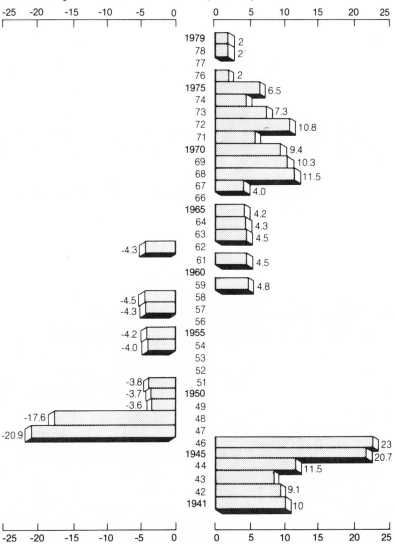

Source: U.S., Department of Commerce, Bureau of the Census

turbing as the recent past. An examination of the statistics on significant factors in American divorce would support this optimistic conclusion about the future stability of the family.

Repeated investigations have found that divorce and marital separation are not evenly distributed throughout the country, but are a function of identifiable demographic, social, and economic characteristics. Religion and geographic location are also factors. For example, while the divorce rate among Catholics has been growing, it remains under the rate for other religious groups. Meanwhile, divorce rates in the western states tend to be far higher than those in the east.[16]

Individuals with low incomes and in the lower levels of the socioeconomic hierarchy experience more than their share of marital disruptions. This may account in part for the much higher divorce rates among nonwhites than among whites. Lower educational attainment also strongly increases the probability that marriage will wind up in divorce. It is difficult to give a specific weight to each of these various factors. However, some researchers have concluded that income variables have a much stronger impact on marriage stability than educational attainment and occupational factors.[17] But there are indications that stability of income and employment, even more than the amount of earned income, plays a major role in the divorce decision.[18]

Family analysts' views of the role of children in preserving a marriage have undergone some radical changes in recent years. The debate persists as to whether couples have children because they intend to stay together or whether having children keeps them from seeking a divorce. The traditional view has been that the birth of a child often stabilizes a shaky marriage. As one analyst in the 1930s put it, "Clearly, children hold their parents together."[19] However, recent research using longitudinal data indicates that the impact of children on divorce is far more complex. On average, couples having serious marital problems tend to postpone bringing children into the world. One study found that marital separation is much less likely among couples with preschool children. But such couples often merely postpone separation until the youngsters reach school age.

It has been argued that laws which make it easier to untie the marriage knot, including "no-fault divorce laws," have encouraged people to end their marriages. Some studies of state data have shown a high correlation between the ease of obtaining a divorce and the probability that couples will seek to end their marriage. However, a study of conditions before and after the institution of California's no-fault divorce law in 1969 indicated that the law did not affect the general trend of divorce in that state. These findings imply that easier divorce laws are just as much a governmental response to shifts in social mores as their cause.[20]

It is difficult to forecast the future of divorce rates. To some extent, divorce rates follow marriage rates. Roughly half of the divorces after first marriage occur during the first seven years, and about half of the divorces after remarriage occur during the first three years. There is roughly a four- to six-year lag between the rise in marriage and divorce rates. The increase in divorce rates of the late 1960s and early 1970s followed earlier, albeit smaller, increases in marriage rates. As the marriage rate appears to have peaked, the divorce rate probably will not continue to grow at an accelerating pace. The recent trend to delay the first marriage, with fewer teenagers and people in their early twenties entering into marriage, should contribute to greater marriage stability in the 1980s. Also, there will be a decline in the number of teenagers and people in their early twenties, which will further reduce divorce rates in the years ahead.

Some of the most interesting variables and factors in marriage and divorce decisions are the hardest for social scientists to capture. Statistical model builders can feed their computers only so-called hard data—like income and educational attainment—and must ignore nonquantifiable institutional forces that might be the most important factors affecting change.

It might be argued that divorce feeds on itself in a way that model builders find difficult to capture in their equations. Divorce appears to have gained a far wider acceptance as a socially approved solution to marital conflicts, and religious constraints are playing a diminishing role. Also, when considering divorce, a husband and wife might weigh the chances of finding a replacement for the about-to-be discarded mate. With a low divorce rate, the pool of eligible new partners would tend to be small, whereas a higher divorce rate would expand the pool. Labor market conditions should also be considered. As married women achieve a greater degree of financial independence from men, fewer may wish to remain with their present husbands, and those who work with other men may want to extend the relationship from a work bench or office desk to the home. The rapid growth of women in the labor force may therefore continue to influence family dissolutions, undermining any stabilization in the divorce rate. Sound projections about divorce rates in the 1980s remain elusive, and the data can be used to "prove" the projector's biases.

Remarriage

Just as quitting a job does not mean leaving the labor force, divorce does not mean a permanent withdrawal from the marriage arena. Some 22 percent of all American marriages involve at least one partner who has been previously married, including 6 percent of the brides and 9 percent of the grooms where both partners are repeaters.

The proportion who remarry drops with age. Three of four women whose first marriage ends in divorce before the age of 30 wind up remarried. The comparable rates are almost three out of five for women aged 30 to 39 years and one out of four for women 40 years of age or older.

Having children seems to delay but not prevent women's remarriage. For women under age 30 who remarry, the median number of years between marriages is 2.9 if they have no children; 3.1 if they have one or two children; and 4 if they have three to five children. Similarly, divorced women under age 30 have an 80 percent chance of being remarried if they have no children, but their chance is still above 70 percent if they have three to five children.

Many divorced men cannot long endure their return to bachelorhood. In fact, divorced men are three times more likely to remarry than never-married men are to enter their first marriage. The same social, cultural, and economic factors that play a significant role in first-marriage decisions seem to also influence remarriages. For example, divorced men who have higher incomes and more stable employment patterns are more likely to remarry. There has been a long-run increase in the remarriage rate that tends to mirror shifts in the divorce level. However, during the early 1970s the divorce rate continued to rise while the remarriage rate hit a peak and leveled off. Part of the long-term gains in the remarriage rate among women can be explained by the increased ratio of divorced to widowed women. Divorced women, on average, are more likely than widows to remarry. One result of a leveling off in the remarriage rate has been an increasing number of households headed by women.[21] Since the 1930s the number of American families has more than doubled, but during the same time the number of households headed by women has more than tripled.

For both men and women, divorce seems to reflect the rejection more of a specific partner than of the institution of marriage. However, sifting through the data indicates that a second marriage has less chance of lasting than a first marriage. While two of three first marriages may be expected to last until death, more than three of seven second marriages are likely to expire before one of the partners.

Unmarried Couples

There has been a significant increase in the number of couples reporting that they are living together without being married. Such "living in sin" is not a recent phenomenon as the Bible and other ancient sources attest. But being willing to admit it to government enumerators is a relatively new phenomenon. In 1960 an estimated 439,000 households were made up of unmarried couples. By the end of the 1970s the number of unmarried couples had increased by 150 percent to over 1 million. Despite an increase in the number of couples living together without being married, the number of children in their households has remained about the same. In 1960, roughly 45 percent of all unmarried households contained three or more persons, but by 1979, only about 20 percent of these households contained more than two persons.

Most cohabitation arrangements do not last long, and many of the partners apparently do not view them as permanent. For example, in 1977 about 63 percent of unmarried couples had been living together for less than two years. In earlier years admission of cohabitation before marriage was adequate cause for dismissal from a job and banishment from respectable society. Since then courts have stepped in to protect the rights of unmarried persons living together, and social disapproval has vastly diminished. In 1960 there were good reasons for "sinners" to hide their living arrangements. Two decades later the reasons for such secrecy have weakened.

WEIGHING THE EVIDENCE

Despite the serious jolts experienced by the American family, the majority of marriages do not end in divorce. Most divorced persons seek a new stable relationship. Very few people marry more than twice. Marriage and the family are still viewed by an overwhelming majority of Americans as a proper and apparently preferred living arrangement.

However, all this does not minimize the real changes that have taken place. Current divorce rates are higher than ever. Between 1960 and 1979, the proportion of households not maintained by families as traditionally defined almost doubled—from one in seven to one in four. One-parent families accounted for 13 percent of all households in 1979, up 4 percentage points from 1960.

Nevertheless, a prediction that marriage is due for extinction is not in order—not yet. However, if marriage vows were dictated by

"We were married in 1964, 1974 and 1980."

recorded facts, at least one-third of marrying couples would change the promise "until death" to "until we change partners." Still, living as part of a family seems to be the preference of most adult Americans—and they like to play for keeps and to make it "legal." The increase in the number of unmarried couples seems to be more of a way station than a final refuge in life. Despite a permissive society's toleration of experimentation, most individuals seem to prefer the traditional contractual relationship with all its obligations and restraints.

It is hard to judge whether society is better or worse off under these relaxed conditions than it was in an earlier puritanical era. The buffeting to which the family has been subjected has generated tensions and scars that have led many to psychiatrists' couches, and many more victims did not have the resources to tell their woes to the would-be mental healers. It may be argued that being forced to live in an unhappy and destructive marriage is a worse evil than a divorce. But as long as society condones that solution, individuals are in a position to make a free choice. The challenge is whether Americans will use their new-found freedoms wisely.

For now, it appears that the family is withstanding the changes produced by the new social freedoms. However, the surviving institution will demonstrate many basic differences from previous and more traditional patterns.

Chapter Three

BE FRUITFUL AND MULTIPLY

> And God blessed them; and God said unto them: "Be fruitful and multiply. . . ." And they were both naked, the man and his wife, and they were not ashamed.
>
> Genesis 1:28, 2:25

> Every man must marry a wife in order to beget children, and he who fails of this duty is as one who sheds blood, diminishes the Image of God, and causes the Divine Presence to depart from Israel.
>
> Shulchan Aruch

NEW CONCEPTIONS

Religions have played a major role in shaping the family although the approaches dictated by the same faiths over time have varied widely, reflecting changing mores and practices. For example, in the Shulchan Aruch, the basic legal text used by Orthodox Jews in guiding their behavior, the biblical admonition to "be fruitful and multiply" was interpreted to mean not only that couples must marry before they produce progeny, but also as a commandment to marry in order "to multiply." Failure to obey this commandment is considered not only a serious offense to God but also to the entire community.

Similar exhortations and commandments concerning fertility and children can be found in the doctrinal core of most of the world's leading religions. Christianity has placed a strong emphasis on marriage and the resulting offspring. The epistles of the New Testament contain numerous exhortations concerning procreation and "proper"

family life. While husbands and wives are urged to strive for the world to come, they are repeatedly reminded of their earthly duties. In the Mormon church marriage combined with parenthood is considered the best assurance of eternal exaltation, which is not available to man or woman in a single state. The Koran not only tells the Muslims of Allah's great delight in children, but also reveals strict commandments concerning parental responsibilities toward a child's upbringing. Buddhism recognizes many different roads to enlightenment. Some people are called upon to give up having families and to devote their full time to a spiritual awakening. However, the Buddha noted that for others, being parents would become an integral part of their spiritual growth. For Confucius, the way toward obtaining goodness was centrally linked with family relationships and responsibilities.

One of the main functions of a family has been to produce, nurture, and socialize the next generation. While the family does not have to be child oriented, the needs of the young have played a primary role in the evolution of this institution. An old nursery rhyme summed up the traditional mores quite succinctly: "First comes love; then comes marriage; then come children in a baby carriage."

However, in a growing number of cases this conventional order has not been followed. Love often results in just living together—not in marriage. Even if marriage does follow love, the need for the proverbial baby carriage may be long postponed—the result of advanced birth control practices. And since the 1973 Supreme Court ruling, which struck down restrictive state laws regarding abortion—especially during the first three months of pregnancy—legal abortions increasingly have been used as a means of fertility control. In some cases, the baby carriage is never needed. For many adults, the word crib more often is associated with cheating on tests than with a child's bed. With a rise in illegitimate births, the baby carriage—if it can be afforded—has often preceded marriage. In many cases, nuptial vows have not followed the birth.

As more women receive longer education and enter the labor force, motherhood increasingly must vie with their other options or aspirations. Following the post–World War II baby boom, fertility rates have plummeted to historic lows. Many Western countries already have zero population growth, and they are starting to record fertility rates that portend significant population declines. This trend has been viewed with dire alarm by some analysts. According to Norman Podhoretz:

> There can be no more radical refusal of self-acceptance than the repudiation of one's own biological nature; and there can be no abdication of responsibility more fundamental than the refusal of a man to become, and to be, a father, or a woman to become, and to be, a mother. . . . When the plague invaded women as women and men as men, the birth rate began to fall precipitately and the number of abortions soon exceeded the number of births.[1]

However, not all observers are dismayed by the decline in birth rates. Some view the development with equanimity, and even welcome it, because current living conditions are far less spacious than in the Garden of Eden and manna from heaven has been scarce. Fertility declines might prove socially beneficial.

Beyond decisions on whether to bring children into this world, there remains the problem of who will provide for, and socialize, them once they are born. Under traditional social mores and legal sanctions, the answer to these questions was the family. However, as the number of separations, divorces, and out-of-wedlock births has increased, the answers have been changing. These changes have had a dramatic impact not only on the structure of the family, but also on the role of the state in modern society. The ways in which American society and families cope with these changes could well determine the future viability of the family and the direction of the modern welfare state.

Fertility Patterns

Demographers have developed several different ways to measure annual fertility rates. The *crude birth rate* records the number of births per 1,000 population, while the *general fertility rate* considers only the childbearing portion of the population by counting the number of births per 1,000 women between 15 and 44 years old. Finally, the *total fertility rate* measures the annual fertility of 1,000 women over the course of their reproductive lives based on the rates characteristic of various age groups. In order to maintain zero population growth, females must sustain a total fertility rate of 2.1—rather than 2—because not all of them survive to the reproduction ages or are fertile.

In its early years, the United States had a higher total fertility rate than many European nations.[2] While early data are fragmentary, the

FIGURE 4.

Following the post–World War II baby boom, the American birthrate for both whites and blacks has resumed its historic decline.

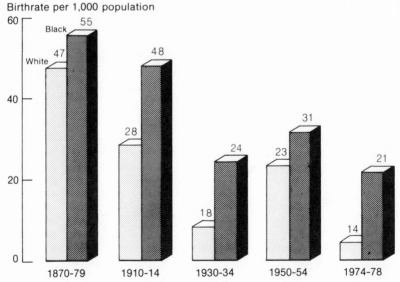

Birthrate per 1,000 population

Source: U.S., Department of Commerce, Bureau of the Census

crude birth rate in the United States appears to have been about 50 per 1,000 population in 1800.[3] Thereafter, the American birth rate declined fairly steadily until World War II. The postwar "baby boom" lasted until the early 1960s, when the birth rate resumed its secular decline, plummeting to 15 per 1,000 by the close of the 1970s.

Not only have women tended to postpone marriage, reducing the number of years available for legitimate births—which is still the prevailing, if old-fashioned, standard—but they also have deferred becoming mothers after they do marry. The median interval between a first marriage and the birth of the first child rose from about 15 months in the early 1960s to over 2 years during the late 1970s. By the third year of marriage only about one of five women in their first marriage was still childless during the early 1960s, compared with roughly three of seven by the end of the succeeding decade. The number of births expected or desired by women also fell sharply, from 3.1 in 1965 to 2.3 in 1978 among wives 18 to 34 years old, and by the latter year the average for wives 18 to 24 years of age was only 2.1, or roughly the zero population growth level.[4]

As analysts tend to base their predictions of fertility rates on historic trends, it is important to consider both the long-run and short-term fluctuations of these statistics (figure 4). Current fertility rates take on more meaning when they are placed in historical perspective.

Baby Booms and Busts

The Great Depression of the 1930s brought a major reduction in American fertility levels. With the nation in dire economic circumstances, many adults put off marriage, and many of those who did marry decided that they could not afford as many extra mouths to feed as in the past. Given these conditions, the birth rate plummeted to about 18 per 1,000 by 1933, and it remained under 23 per 1,000 during World War II.

At the end of the war, many American adults decided to make up for lost time, and a new baby boom was on at full speed. From a low of 2.4 million births in the depth of the depression and 2.9 million in the final year of World War II, births in the United States rose to a peak of 4.3 million in 1957. Since then, the annual number of births has declined almost continuously, reaching a low of 3.1 million in 1975, but then rising slowly to 3.3 million three years later.

All three measures of fertility have shown major reductions since

FIGURE 5.

Women of all ages have shown a marked decline in fertility since the baby boom.

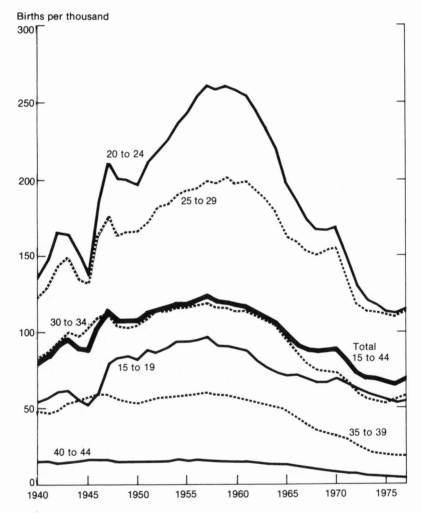

Source: National Center for Health Statistics

the peak of the baby boom in 1957. The fertility decline is even more pronounced when the shifts in the age structure of the American population are considered. The crude fertility rate fell by about 40 percent between 1957 and 1978. During the same period, the total fertility rate, which considers age characteristics of the population, was cut in half. The general fertility rate was in between the two, and it indicated roughly a 46 percent drop during this period. Women of all ages have shown a marked decline in fertility since the baby boom (figure 5). Women in the older childbearing years have recently shown a slight increase in their fertility rate, indicating that many females who postponed motherhood are deciding that it is either now or never.

While the U.S. total fertility rate closed the 1970s at about 1.8 and was well under the 2.1 zero population growth level, the size of the total American population will not decline in the twentieth century. Despite birth rate declines, births still outnumbered deaths by 1.5 million during 1979. Also, the United States continued to serve as a haven for immigrants fleeing either persecution or poverty in their native countries. Most of these immigrants have been young adults. Population bulges, like the post–World War II baby boom, are like a boa constrictor digesting its prey. The age-cohort bulges can be tracked as their ramifications are evolving. The postwar baby boom resulted in a surfeit of women whose childbearing years span the period from about 1960 to about 2000—long enough to sustain a growth in the native American population for several decades. It will take about 65 years for the American population to stabilize at zero population growth even if current rates hold firm.[5] If one assumes that the total fertility rate will nudge down to 1.7, the American population would not stop growing until about the year 2015, when it would reach approximately 250 million people—an 11 percent growth in 35 years. If the total fertility rate would jump back to 2.1, the American population would be about 260 million in the year 2000 and 283 million in 2015. Both levels are considerably lower than the 300 million population prediction for the year 2000, which until quite recently was the ballpark estimate given by many reputable demographers.[6]

The United States is far from unique in these fertility rate trends, and a reduced birth rate seems to be shared by most industrialized nations regardless of whether their economic and social structure is a capitalistic welfare state or a communist regime. While international comparisons can be misleading, it appears that in the 1970s the United States continued to experience a higher birth rate than many other industrialized countries (figure 6).

FIGURE 6.

U.S. fertility has exceeded
that of most other major
industrial countries.

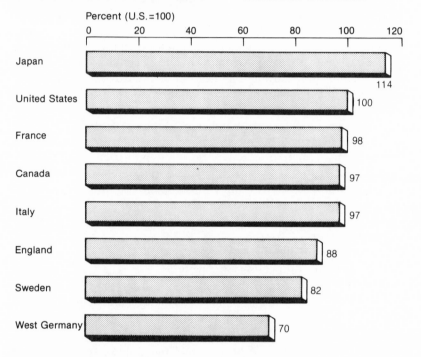

Source: U.S., Department of Commerce, Bureau of the Census

Lower birth rates seem to have caused far more public concern
in European countries than in the United States.[7] For example, West
Germany's native population has been falling steadily since 1972,
with annual deaths exceeding births. Given the present course, the
German native population will fall to 52 million by the year 2000,
a 9 percent decline in less than one generation. In several Eastern
European nations, abortion laws have been made stricter.

The uneven swings in the U.S. birth rate since the 1930s have
already affected the age distribution of the American population
(figure 7). In 1920 the age configuration of the population looked
very much like a pyramid. The largest group of the population was
children under 10 years of age, who formed the base of the population pyramid. At that time, each successive age group was smaller
than the one preceding it.

FIGURE 7.

Wide variations in the birthrate have changed the age profile of the American population.

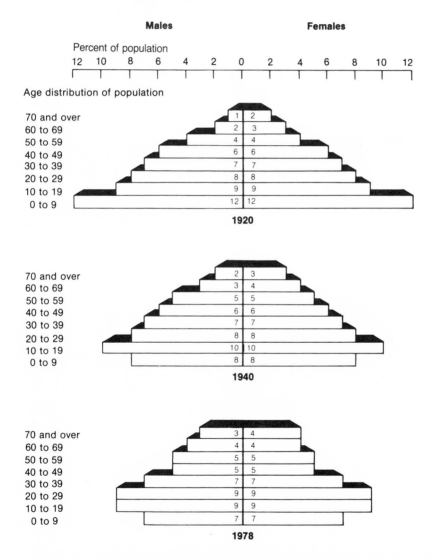

Source: U.S., Department of Commerce, Bureau of the Census

However, with steep fertility declines during the 1930s—followed by continued low birth rates during World War II—the percentage of children under age 10 declined. Then came the baby boom, which was succeeded by the renewed birth rate declines. By the end of the 1970s, the profile was far from the simple triangular shape depicted half a century earlier. Several relatively small birth cohorts are now sandwiched in between far larger groups, so the profile resembles a tiered cake put together by an amateur. If current fertility trends continue—coupled with a longer life expectancy—the American population profile could look more like an inverted pyramid. Smaller and younger birth cohorts would be supporting a far larger and topheavy structure represented by an increasing number of older Americans. The changing relative composition of the age cohorts has created wide variations and imbalances between the demands of successive birth cohorts for educational facilities, health care, and provisions for the aged. It also has placed uneven strains on American labor markets as birth cohorts reach successive stages in their work lives.

FUTURE TRENDS

Based on the assumption that the past is prologue to the future, social scientists have long attempted to predict fertility rates and population trends. They have used a wide range of different models, which incorporate numerous demographic, social, and economic assumptions. It shouldn't be surprising that the predictions on fertility rates have not converged on any one path.

The track record of fertility predictions leaves much to be desired. Many analysts predicted continued low birth rates—and even close to zero population growth—following World War II. Actually, fertility levels skyrocketed. Perhaps the best known miscalculation on population trends was made in the early 1800s by Thomas Malthus. In his famous essay on population, Malthus predicted that human reproduction would increase at a geometric pace while food supplies would lag way behind since they could only grow in a much slower arithmetic progression.[8] Events in the leading industrialized nations—including fertility patterns, major productivity increases, and family planning—did not follow the course outlined by Malthus. In fact, for the United States, agricultural productivity has outstripped human fertility.

A New Boom?

The numerous misses have not discouraged analysts from projecting fertility rates, although the tools keep changing. In recent years advanced statistical research methods and computers have replaced gut feelings and crystal balls. One current school of thought does not view the recent dearth of births as a lasting phenomenon, anticipating a significant upswing in the birth rate starting in the 1980s and continuing well into the 1990s.

Representative of this view is research conducted by three University of Pennsylvania economists—Richard Easterlin, Michael Wachter, and Susan Wachter. Their hypothesis is that the birth rate is a function of the size of the birth cohort currently within the childbearing years. As individuals of a small birth cohort mature, they tend to face relatively little competition from their peers, compared with the intense struggle faced by members of a large birth cohort. Because their numbers are low, they have an easier time gaining admittance to a desired college, university, or vocational training program. When they enter the labor force, members of the small birth cohort experience little difficulty in finding entry-level positions; and they can establish themselves fairly quickly. As a result, they will be in better financial position, and they will be able to afford an early marriage and more children. The net impact of all these advantages is an increase in the birth rate.[9]

Members of a large birth cohort will face opposite conditions; it will be harder for them to receive the desired education and training, and the competition for entry-level positions will be intensified. Therefore, they will take much more time in establishing themselves and will postpone marriage, and the birth rate will tend to fall.

Backers of this analysis believe that it explains both the 1946–57 rise in fertility rates and the subsequent baby bust. A small birth cohort hit the labor market following the Great Depression and World War II and they found a strong demand for their services in the labor market. Their economic prospects were so much brighter than the expectations that had been formed in the 1930s that they were willing to marry early and raise large families. However, the experiences of the next birth cohort were very different, as the products of the baby boom faced tough competition from early childhood, and as the supply of qualified workers vastly expanded, individuals who lacked advanced training or skills faced bleak employment prospects. Because this birth cohort's prospects were far less rosy than their parents', they tended to postpone marriage and vastly reduce the number of children per family. Hence, the baby boom bubble burst.

If the latter hypothesis is correct, the cycle is about to repeat itself with another fertility upswing; though in all probability it will be smaller than the original postwar baby boom. Granted this next generation will be in the economic position to have more children, the question is: Will they want them?

Charles Westoff of Princeton University's Office of Population Research is a leading representative of analysts who believe that in the near future birth rates below the zero population growth level may prove to be irreversible. It appears that women who entered the labor force are there to stay. The diffusion of sophisticated bedroom and household technology, combined with changing female aspirations and attitudes, has eased the transition into the labor force for many women. This factor will hold down the fertility rate. Coupled with these conditions are a record number of divorced women who head their households. Also, inflationary pressures mean that a growing number of families require two pay checks to maintain the standard of living to which they are accustomed and to do a little better. The net result is that the proportion of all American women in the prime childbearing years who work outside the home rose from less than two of five in 1960 to roughly three of five by the end of the 1970s. In fact, according to this school, instead of rising, the American fertility rate may even decline from the already low level of about 1.8.

Analysts who predict a new baby boom counter these arguments by noting that by the end of World War II women were in the labor force at what were then record numbers, and they were, on average, better educated than males of the same age. Despite these factors, and a taste of financial independence, fertility rates increased following the war. Also, there still exists a significant earnings gap between men and women. Women still must work eight days to gross the same amount of earnings as men do in five days. In 1979 the median annual earnings of full-time male workers was $17,061 compared with $10,167 for women. The differential has remained at about this level since 1961, despite women's employment gains. In fact, the gap is even wider than it was in 1955, when women earned about 64 percent as much as males compared with 60 percent in 1979.[10]

A small birth cohort during the next generation could result in improved financial security for men. This factor, combined with continued female-male earning gaps and a resumption of earlier productivity trends, could bolster the fertility rate, as more men would be able to afford marriage and children at a younger age. And women with lower income potentials may want the security represented by marriage. However, this theory can be stood on its head to produce the exact opposite result. If the demand for labor grows faster than the labor supplied by this smaller cohort, then wages will tend to rise and more employers will hire women. Also, the enforcement of equal rights laws proscribing discrimination in pay will make work for women more lucrative. These factors would tend to induce more women to enter the labor force, and it could reduce their birth expectations. Also, many women have gained employment in the service sector of the economy, which is hospitable toward part-time employment.

The increase in female labor force participation rates already may be having an impact on fertility as it responds to cyclical economic fluctuations. Fertility rates have tended to move in the same direction as swings in the business cycle, rising during economic booms and declining during economic recessions. Now, however, as female labor force participation rises, fertility rates may be moving in a countercyclical fashion. The explanation of this shift may be in the opportunity costs—foregoing the income she would have earned by being employed outside the home—of having children. Women who can earn higher wages in the labor market will tend to have fewer children, other factors being equal, because the opportunity cost of their time is greater. A cyclical upswing expands employment opportunities and raises wages for women. The net result is a fertility rate that moves in a countercyclical fashion—contrary to the traditional pattern—as more women enter a booming labor market. This analysis suggests that as long as women's real wages continue to rise and a large proportion of females are in the labor force, the fertility rate could remain low.[11]

FAMILY STRUCTURE

Whatever the future of the fertility rate, the important questions center on its impact on the structure of the family. The assumption that a low birth rate reflects either a rejection of children or a weakening of the family does not stand up under close scrutiny. A smaller number of children per household can improve the quality of family life, and it may enable parents to provide better child care.

Smaller Families

The decrease in total fertility rates has not been due to any statistically significant increase in childlessness, but rather to a rapid decline in the number of women who have experienced four or more births. Of the women born in 1870, nearly half had four or more children and about one-fifth had none.By comparison among women born in 1925, one-third had four or more children and only one-tenth remained childless. The cohort of current young women who are potential mothers, of course, has not finished its production of children. In the meantime, statistics on birth expectations can be used as a rough estimate of the fertility distribution for women born during the baby boom. If these expectations prove to be in the ball-park, the current crop of young women will continue this smaller family trend. Of the wives born between 1952 and 1958, 4 of 7 can be expected to have two children, 1 of 14 to have four or more, and only 1 of 18 to remain childless.[12] Only about 1 of 10 women in the 1870 birth cohort, and 1 of 4 in the 1925 birth cohort, had only two children. The major trend does not appear to be toward childlessness.[13] Instead, couples are using the pill and other means of birth control, including abortion, to limit the number of children they have.

"We have a small family . . . just Bob, me and the hamster."

While some women who enter the labor force may decide not to have any children, recent medical advances have helped many women become pregnant and overcome gynecological problems that formerly prevented childbearing. In the past, a good portion of the married women remained childless because of medical difficulties. While labor force participation by women may encourage some to remain childless, medical advances offering couples the choice of having children have worked to counteract this trend.

The mixing of work outside the home and childbearing are becoming increasingly the norm, although labor force participation apparently tends to defer motherhood. In 1978, one-third of married women (between the ages of 18 and 34) who gave birth during the year were in the labor force, and among employed married women in this age group, approximately three of seven were also mothers. Between 1955 and 1975, the proportion of married women between the ages of 20 and 24 who were childless rose from 33 percent to almost 43 percent. However, among married women between the ages of 25 and 29, the proportion without children was virtually the same in both years (20 percent). Added education does tend to discourage motherhood. Females 18 to 34 years old with one or more years of college are childless at about twice the rate of non–high school graduates—14 and 7 percent, respectively.[14]

Predicting size of families on the basis of expectations is no less hazardous than most projections. There is many a slip between expectations and the actual number of births. Morever, until the mid-1970s, the Bureau of the Census gathered data only from married women about their future family plans. Given the growing number of births outside of marriage, the birth expectations and actual fertility rates of unmarried women could have a strong impact on the size of the average American household.

Quality, Not Quantity

The reduction in the size of the average American family can provide positive benefits that could improve the quality of life for both children and parents.While participation in the labor force is not inherently incompatible with motherhood for a growing number of women, it does seem to induce a reduction in family size. The women's liberation movement has made some inroads on the allocation of family chores, yet child care in a majority of families is still mostly the mother's responsibility—and it seems that many mothers still do not get significant help in these chores from other

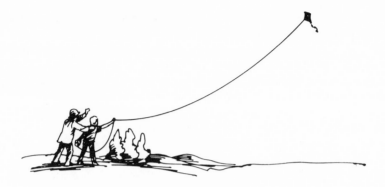

family members.[15] In order to enter the labor force, a growing number of women seem to have opted for having fewer children.

One major advance in the investigation of families was made possible by a longitudinal study conducted by the University of Michigan's Survey Research Center. This survey tracked over 5,000 American families for the five years ending in 1972. The results indicated that the number of children can have a strong impact on the quality of family life.

Being a highly subjective concept, the impact of the number of children on the quality of family life is difficult to measure. Furthermore, the data on family life are very meager, so analysts are forced to use proxies and simulations.

One fairly obvious impact of the number of children on the quality of family life is that large families are often destitute because their income cannot support so many members, even if their income is substantial. And even one child can push a low income family into proverty.[16] For example, an annual income of $20,000 represents a per capita income of $5,000 for a family of four, but only $4,000 for a family of five.

One proxy used to measure the subjective notion of quality was educational attainment. Education affects an individual's future occupational opportunities, earnings, and ability to land a job that also provides a high degree of personal satisfaction. It was felt that educational attainment might be one rough measure of the quality and quantity of resources received by each child within a family. One hypothesis that was tested predicted that sharing family time and money with siblings would reduce a child's achievement level; all other factors being equal, as the family size increases the schooling expected for each sibling would be reduced. The model employed in this study emphasized that a larger family size tends to strain the parents' ability to devote time, energy, and money to each child. Family size had a stronger negative impact on educational attainment for females than for males. For both boys and girls the most important influence on educational attainment was the size of parental income. As expected, the higher the parental income, the more education a child tended to receive. But the data also suggested that a larger number of siblings can adversely affect their test scores.[17] Other studies on intrafamily sibling differences in educational attainment have reached similar conclusions. In fact, it appears that family size is even a more important determinant of the schooling received per child than the birth order and spacing of siblings.[18]

On the other hand, some have suggested that the impact of added children may be exaggerated and that economies of scale apply to the quality of family life. Running the washer to clean several children's clothes instead of one child's probably adds little marginal costs. A story can be read to two children as well as to one. Cooking and shopping burdens might not grow proportionately as the number of children increases. But the implications of economies of scale to the production of children have been questioned. The University of Michigan analysts used the economy of scale hypothesis to explore the allocation of resources and the time inputs devoted to childrearing by its sample of families. They concluded that the time devoted to preschool children did not diminish significantly as their number increased within a family, but in low-status families (defined by income and the occupation of the household head) the quality level (as measured in the study) given to each child suffered.[19]

Other data also back up this finding that the added burden of additional children is not totally counteracted by economies of scale. It might be argued that as a family becomes more affluent, it can afford to purchase more services outside of the household to help reduce the burden of childrearing. Because other people would be paid to take on some of the chores of childrearing, parents with high incomes would not have to invest so much of their own time in having larger families. While affluent parents might be able to afford this method of childrearing, apparently many of them have not chosen this route; in fact, they devote to each preschool child about twice as many total housework hours as do low-status families. Of course, part of this difference reflects a tendency for affluent families to have fewer children than low-income families. As wealthier parents appear to be very concerned about the quality of care received by their children, raising larger families demands a major investment of their time.[20] Also, given the high cost of domestic and child-care services, even many wealthier families find financing such services to be a major problem.

Part of the economic burden for larger households would be mitigated if employers or the state took family size into consideration when establishing compensation levels for employees. Most industrial countries provide family allowances to ease the burden of child-rearing (and also to increase the population). But in most countries these allowances are inadequate to significantly affect childrearing. However, except for dependents' deductions allowed by the tax system, the United States compensation system fails to take into consideration the number of dependents for whom a worker may be responsible.[21]

Children may take on a different status depending upon the number of children in the family. The economist's concept of marginal utility can help explain this phenomenon. The first automobile, or other commodity, purchased by a family tends to have a higher marginal utility—or value—as far as the family is concerned than a second or third. The smaller the number of children, the more each child will be treasured and the greater the resources that can be allocated to each.

Higher-income families may find it easier to provide quality resources to more children compared to lower-income families, but on the average the former have brought fewer children into the world compared to the latter. However, women not in the labor force have shown a U-shaped fertility curve in recent years as women in the middle-income groups have recorded the lowest fertility rates. All other factors being equal, two-wage-earner families tend to have fewer children compared to one-wage-earner families.

Family Life Cycles

Shifting fertility and mortality rates, coupled with changes in birth spacing intervals, have had a strong impact on family life cycle patterns in America. The birth spacing intervals between marriage and the first birth, or between the first birth and the second birth, have become longer. The interval between the second and third births lengthened by more than six months between the first half of the 1960s and the end of the 1970s, and an increasing proportion of women never gave birth to a third child.

Meanwhile, with increased life expectancy and barring divorce, a husband and wife could expect to spend many more years together before one of them died. And most of the added years would occur after their children had left the home. For couples married in 1900, one partner (more often the husband) was likely to meet his or her Maker almost at the same time the last child left home. The average age of a mother when her last child marries has fallen throughout this century. Together, these changes have added more than 11 "empty nest," or child-free, years at the end of the typical husband and wife life cycle since 1900. At the same time, couples, on average, have postponed having their first child. Adding these child-free years into the total, the couple now can expect to spend about 13 years together without any children. Given an average of 44 years of married life for couples who carry out the vows of "until death," it appears that couples now entering marriage can expect to spend almost 30 percent of their time together without any children in their home.[22]

In short, changes in the fertility and mortality rates have had a radical impact on the nature as well as the length of family life cycles. The adult family life cycle now has been almost divided into two separate periods: the first period is the one in which children are born and raised to adulthood; the second period is one where parents live apart from their children. Perhaps, this phenomenon can also help explain why childlessness has not increased. Even those couples who do experience the joys of parenthood also can expect many child-free years together.

BEING FRUITFUL

Adults today are not following the first commandment God gave to Adam and Eve with the same zeal shown by past generations. The fertility rate has fallen to a historic low in America, and a similar trend has been experienced in almost every other advanced industrialized nation. In the United States, the decline in fertility does not reflect any increase in childlessness. Rather, a decreasing proportion of women are spending their prime childbearing years exclusively as baby producers adding work outside the home to the responsibilities of motherhood. A household with four or more children increasingly has become a rarity.

As the burden of childrearing is diminishing, parents can boost the resources devoted per child, and even low-income families may be able to improve (with government help) the quality of childrearing. Though fewer in relative number, children may become even more cherished within families and by society at large.

Family planning and solutions to medical problems that once

blocked fertility are providing adults with many more options about being fruitful and multiplying. Multiplying, however, is a blessing only if the children produced are wanted by their parents. Being fruitful now seems to include greater consideration for opportunities offered to the children as well as to their parents—including for many women the rewards received from employment as well as motherhood. As more women seek employment outside the home, a growing number of men and children will have to assume greater responsibility in the daily chores of family life. This breakdown in sexual stereotyped roles could have a very positive influence on improving life within American households.

A declining population growth rate requires diverse social and economic adjustments. Shifting American fertility rates have altered the age profile of the nation's population, and, combined with changes in mortality rates, the average family life cycle now shows a different pattern from the past. The size of the U.S. population is going to grow, albeit at a slower rate, for many years before the annual number of deaths exceeds the yearly number of births and net migration gains. Moreover, fertility patterns do not appear to be immune from active governmental human resource policies, and there appears to be sufficient lead time to adjust and formulate "pronatalist" programs if the need arises and if public policy deems it wise. However, given the current state of the art and social scientists' knowledge about fertility decisions, policymakers are a long way from being able to "fine tune" the birth rate, and it is to be hoped that they will not attempt to achieve such a questionable goal.

Chapter Four

THE CARE AND FEEDING OF CHILDREN

"My dear, sweet Billy:
Mommy has gone away. Sometimes in the world,
daddys go away and the mommys bring up their little
boys. But sometimes a mommy can go away, too, and
you have your daddy to bring you up. . . . Listen to
your daddy. He will be like your wise Teddy.
Love, Mommy . . ."

"Mommy went away?"
"Yes, Billy."
"Forever, Daddy?"
Avery Corman, *Kramer versus Kramer*

A HOUSE DIVIDED

An unhappy family life and a broken home are often assumed to create even more trauma and lasting scars for the children involved than for the husband and wife. This is not to minimize the suffering experienced by a rejected spouse, because the anger, fear, recrimination, and self-doubt can be destructive. For children, however, the problem may be exacerbated if their family disintegrates when they are in the sensitive periods of their early development.

The traditional family model pictures a child as being raised by both natural mother and father, providing guidance, protection, and socialization. Even under ideal circumstances, growing up with two loving parents is a difficult job. As the annual crop of divorces has

57

increased, relatively more children are being raised by only one of their natural parents. And with remarriages, even many children who have two adults in the house are not living with both their natural mother and father. Added to divorces and broken homes, illegitimate births have remained a significant social factor; they now account for roughly one of every seven births in the United States. Clearly, the family with only one parent in the house has become an all too frequent phenomenon on the American scene.

Whether a married couple should remain together or seek a divorce would seem to be a private matter between two adults. However, the large number of children involved raises a whole host of sensitive and difficult problems that can have a major impact upon the rest of society. Family breakup and the absence of one or both parents raises numerous deep-seated concerns: Who will raise the next generation and socialize it, and what role and responsibilities should society—either through the public or private sectors—undertake? Will the products of broken homes create massive problems for educational, judicial, and social welfare institutions?

A chief concern centers on what will happen when children raised in single-parent households come of age to form their own families. Will the lack in childhood of a stable two-parent family prove to be an insurmountable roadblock for many individuals in the next generation's efforts to form such lasting ties? After viewing their divorced parents' difficulties and the consequent punishment visited upon the children, many young adults may sour on the family and try different alternatives to marriage and the two-parent family. If this is the case, the problem of broken homes could become self-perpetuating and self-sustaining from one generation to the next.

Care and Custody

Social pressures to keep a marriage going if children are involved have diminished. More than five of seven adults now believe that it is socially permissible for a married couple to get a divorce when they cannot get along—even if they have children. At the same time, the vast majority of American adults also believe that a child raised by one parent in a broken home will face many added difficulties. Almost two of three people surveyed believe that coming from a broken home will have a bad effect on a child's education. In reality the choice is often not between a happy and stable two-parent family or having children raised in a one-parent family. Instead, the Hobson's choice is between a marriage that has turned into a battlefield—with the children caught between the trenches—

and being raised by a single parent, more often the mother. Even given these harsh alternatives, fewer than 1 of 20 American adults believe that being raised by only one parent, compared with an unhappy household, will have a positive effect on a child's education.[1]

Often it is not at all clear who will raise and provide for the children under current conditions. As so aptly depicted by Avery Corman in *Kramer versus Kramer*, the established legal provisions regulating child custody are being challenged. At one time under English Common Law, the father was assumed to have almost absolute rights over his children. Legal divorce was rare, and the vast majority of single-parent households arose from the death of a spouse. As divorce became more frequent, the law shifted to give mothers preference in child-custody cases. In America, by the early part of the twentieth century, this preference in favor of the mother almost had become absolute. In most states, the only way a father could win child-custody rights over the mother was by proving to the court that his former spouse was seriously delinquent in her behavior as a mother. This legal doctrine has been undergoing significant changes in recent years that have made it easier for a father to win child custody. However, few children are currently raised by only their male parent. In some states, courts have awarded joint custody to both divorced parents. The entire issue of family law remains unsettled and in a sharp state of flux.

But even if child custody has been determined, there still remains the thorny issue of who will provide the finances to raise the children. Bringing up a child, as any parent will testify, is becoming increasingly expensive. While estimates vary, it costs at least $100,000 (in 1980 prices) for a middle-income family to raise a child from birth through four years of college in a state university. Besides any psychic trauma, members of broken homes headed by females often experience severe economic hardship. One of every seven families in the United States is headed by a woman; for blacks, this rate is approximately 40 percent. About 1 in 3 of these female-headed families live in poverty, compared to 1 in 18 husband-wife families. Almost 17 percent of all American children now live in families headed by a woman.

Even if a mother receives child-support payments, amounts too often tend to be very small. Many fathers fail to provide any child support, and enforcement of their legal obligations has proven to be difficult. For example, Michigan apparently makes more vigorous efforts to enforce child support than any other state and jails one of every seven divorced fathers who fail to make adjudicated child-support payments. Given the poor record of state-operated systems and the widespread incidence of nonsupport, some advocate wage deductions for child support administered by the federal government. Congress has not actively considered this proposal and the number of parents who fail to support their children continues to rise.

Broken Homes

As the divorce rate has increased, the number of children affected by a marital separation also has grown annually (figure 8). Divorces involve each year more than 1 million children under 18 years of age. Toward the end of the 1970s, about 45 percent of all divorcing couples did not have any children under the age of 18, and 11 percent of the divorces involved three or more children. This compares with the mid-1960s, when 37 percent of divorcing couples had no children under 18 years of age, and 20 percent involved three or more children. As a result, the average number of children per divorce decree has declined from a high of 1.34 in 1968 to the current level of 1.01 child per decree.[2]

Fertility declines have helped mitigate the number of children affected by divorce, but the number has more than tripled since the mid-1950s. Hence, while 6.5 per 1,000 children under 18 years of age were involved annually in a divorce in the mid-1950s, the comparable proportion had risen to 18 per 1,000 two decades later. However, this rate may be stabilizing at about current levels, although there is no immediate prospect that the number of children affected by divorce will fall back to the older—and some would say safer—pattern experienced prior to the 1960s.

Consequently, the proportion of children who live with two parents has declined significantly. Nearly all children under 18 years of age still live with one or both of their parents. About 3 percent live with a grandparent or other close relatives. Back in 1960, roughly seven of eight children lived with two parents; now this proportion is down to under four of five.

This change has even been more dramatic for black children under 18 than for whites. Almost as many black children currently live with only their mother as with two parents; while 84 percent of white children live with two parents, only 44 percent of all black children do so. The proportion of one-parent families is much higher for black than for white children (44 percent and 14 percent respectively).[3] As a result, of course, the number of children who live

FIGURE 8.

Both the number and proportion of children involved in a divorce have increased from year to year, while the average number of children per decree has declined.

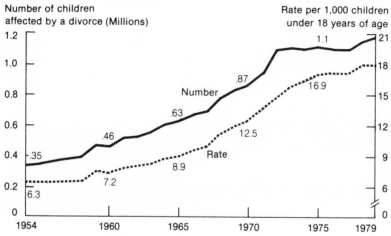

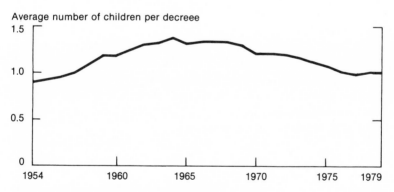

Source: National Center for Health Statistics

with only one parent has grown dramatically. Back in 1960 only about 9 percent of all children lived with only one parent; now almost 19 percent of all children have only one parent in the house.

However, statistics on children who live with two parents do not reveal all of the underlying changes in family structure. Just because

FIGURE 9.

Two of three children are living with their natural parents (1978).

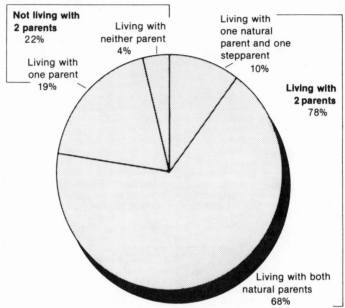

Source: U.S., Department of Commerce, Bureau of the Census

a child has two parents in the house, it does not follow that they are the same two adults who were the child's natural parents. Divorce and remarriage patterns have greatly complicated the picture (figure 9). The chances that a child will not live with two parents increases significantly as a child matures. About 12 percent of infants (under 3 years) do not live with two parents, compared with 20 percent of children aged 14 to 17. About 10 percent of all children under 18 are living with one natural parent and one stepparent, and 67.5 percent of children under 18 years of age are living with their natural fathers and mothers. Well under half of all black children are living with their two parents by birth, both of whom have been married only once, compared with seven-tenths of white children who live in this type of household.[4]

Child-custody laws are undergoing some changes, but more than nine of ten children who live with only one parent still reside in a household headed by their mother. The proportion of all children living with only their mother is about one in six, double the rate two decades earlier. The father's liberation movement notwithstanding, well under 2 percent of all children currently live with only their father. Divorce and marital separation are the prime reasons behind children living with only their mother in roughly two-thirds of the cases, and only about 10 percent of the children in a female-headed household are in this condition because their father died. However, 15 percent of children who live with only their mother do so because their mother has never married.[5]

The vast increase in the proportion of children being raised by only one parent may be jolting. However, before one longs for the "good old days" when separations and divorces were rare, related variables should be considered. At the turn of the century, the chances that a child was not living with any parent were greater than today because many children then were orphans. Even children born between 1911 and 1920 had a 22 percent chance that one of their parents would die before they reached 18 years of age, and they also had a 5 percent chance that their parents would become divorced. Because of improved health conditions, children born in the 1940s faced only a 20 percent chance of losing a parent through either death or divorce. Not until the 1960s did rising divorce rates outweigh the effects of falling death rates on a child's chances of growing up with both parents. As a result, the percentage of children who live with at least one of their natural parents—instead of in institutions, with foster parents, or with other relatives—has been increasing. Still in 1940, about 1 of 10 children did not live with either parent, compared with 1 in about 25 today. While living with one parent instead of with two may not be the best of all possible worlds, this condition would seem to be far preferable to being raised in institutions or by other relatives. A greater number of minority youngsters, compared with white children, live with no parents (8 percent and 2 percent, respectively).[6]

This historical review is not to mitigate current conditions, because the decline in the relative number of two-parent families has the potential for creating many irksome problems. However, it is necessary to have a realistic picture of past conditions for perspective on the present reality. Previous generations had their share of disrupted families although the reasons accounting for the breakups were different than today. While most of the growth of single-parent families is due to increasing trends in marital instability, a significant proportion of the growth is the mirror image of the rapid decline in the number of children who are sent to institutions, foster homes, or relatives.

Children Out of Wedlock

Divorce is only one factor leading to the growth of single-parent families. Some parents do not bother to marry, and about one in seven children in the United States were born out of wedlock in 1978—triple the comparable rate in the mid-1960s. While the number of total births and of legitimate births have declined in recent years, the number of children born to unwed mothers has continued to climb. Currently, over half of all black births and 8 percent of white births are out of wedlock (figure 10).

Teenage girls are the mothers of more than half of the children born out of wedlock each year. Illegitimacy rates for women 20 years and older have declined somewhat due to wider availability and greater acceptance of better contraceptive devices. However, the benefits of modern bedroom technology have not filtered down to many teenage girls. Limited knowledge and use of contraceptive devices, as well as restricted accessibility and the failure to use the devices when they are available, have kept teenage illegitimacy rates at their high level. About 45 percent of premarital pregnancies by white teenage girls in metropolitan areas are aborted compared with 20 percent of those of black teenage girls.[7]

About 10 percent of all females between the ages of 15 and 19 become pregnant annually, accounting for about 600,000 births—including some 250,000 born out of wedlock. After giving birth, the teenage mother—even if she is married—faces the difficult challenge of raising the child. In almost nine of ten cases, the teenage mother decides to keep the child; 8 percent are put up for adoption while the rest are sent to live with other relatives or families.[8] Black teenage mothers on average show a higher propensity to keep their children born out of wedlock than do white teenagers. During pregnancy, almost all of these unmarried teenage mothers live with their families, and nearly half are still living with their families five years after the birth.[9]

Being an unmarried teenage mother has many negative economic and social impacts on the young female as well as the child. These mothers are three times more likely to drop out of school than are teenage girls who are not mothers. Even when family background and other variables that attempt to measure motivation and ability

FIGURE 10.

The proportion and number of
out-of-wedlock births have
grown rapidly.

Percent of out-of-wedlock births

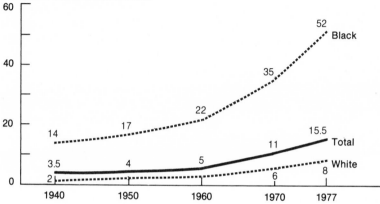

Out-of-wedlock births (thousands)

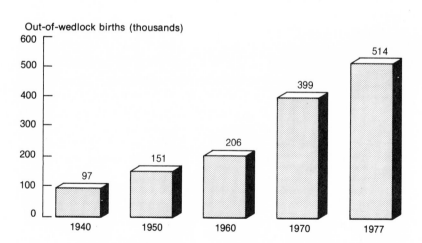

Source: National Center for Health Statistics.

are considered, being an unmarried teenage mother has the statistically significant impact of cutting short a young woman's educational chances. While they may make up part of this educational gap later in life, most of these women will never catch up with those who did not become unwed mothers during their teenage years. Also, becoming an unwed teenage mother increases the chances that a young woman will be living in a poverty household for many years.[10]

As sociologist Arthur Campbell noted, "The girl who has an illegitimate child at the age of 16 suddenly has 90 percent of life's script written for her."[11] In most cases it is a bleak scenario. It will be difficult for her to provide for and raise the child. Her lack of education and other difficulties will make it hard to find and hold a steady, well-paying job. She may feel compelled to marry a man she might not have chosen in different circumstances, and the chances are far greater than average that this marriage will not last.

In fact, there appears to be a direct link between out-of-wedlock births and future divorces leading to broken homes. Four of five women who have premarital births will eventually marry. In many cases of premarital conception, the couple will—voluntarily or under shotgun—marry, and the child will be born after marriage. About one-quarter of the women who entered their first marriage during the period 1970–74 had a first child who was premaritally conceived. Of these women, roughly one-third had the child before marriage, while the remaining two-thirds gave birth during the first eight months following the nuptial vows.[12]

Premarital conception is not new. Historian Richard Lingeman estimated that one-third of the recorded births in Concord, Massachusetts during the two decades prior to the Revolution were conceived out of wedlock. This is roughly the same proportion as in recent years.[13] Whatever the consequence of premarital conceptions in the past, the problem today is that the marriages of women who have a child before the wedding bells sound are far more likely than other marriages to end in early separation or divorce.

Hence, while there is a high probability that a woman who either conceives or bears a child before marriage will wind up with a husband at some time, the probability is also great that she will become a single parent. For the child born prior to the marriage, these circumstances may mean a series of traumatic experiences. The child may first face the world of a one-parent family. If the mother marries, the child for a while may live in a two-parent but unstable household that is likely to be shattered, thus returning the youngster to life in a single-parent household. Next to divorce, out-of-wedlock births have contributed most to the the the decline in the proportion of children who are living in two-parent families.

It is quite difficult to predict with much accuracy the future trend in premarital conceptions and births in the United States. The difficulty stems from conflicting developments. Some evidence suggests that the level of premarital conceptions and births will not grow as rapidly as in the recent past. The improvement and wider dissemination of family planning methods should reduce unwanted conceptions. Also, modern contraceptive devices are being used by more women, even by those who belong to religious groups that proscribe such methods of family planning. Furthermore, though more than half of all illegitimate children have teenage mothers, the peaking of the number of teenage girls in the late 1970s may slow the growth rate for illegitimate births.

Yet, accidents will happen, and the number of unwanted terminated births is likely to depend on the future acceptability and legality of abortions. In 1970—before the Supreme Court decision on abortions—about 1 of 28 pregnancies were legally aborted. Since the legal barriers were lowered, roughly 1 of 5 pregnancies currently result in legal abortions. Although the number of illegal abortions cannot be estimated with any accuracy, it appears that the total number of abortions— illegal as well as legal—has grown rapidly. For lower-income women, government programs to finance abortions have a major impact on whether a pregnancy is terminated. Actions by Congress, sanctioned by the Supreme Court, have cut off federal funding for abortions, except where the mother's life is endangered.

THE IMPACT ON CHILDREN

Frequently the most important issues are the hardest to analyze. The substantial number of single-parent families and the decline in the percentage of children now living with both natural parents are matters of deep concern to American society. The task of evaluating these changes, however, has proven elusive; the social and behavorial sciences have yet to develop a calculus that can even capture—let alone weigh and measure—all of the numerous complex variables.

While the increase in divorces, broken homes, and children born out of wedlock may have many indirect and undetected conse-

quences on the entire population, the consequences for youngsters undergoing family disintegration are major and direct. The proportion of children who live in broken homes has been viewed as an index of social disorganization by Emile Durkheim and more recent observers.

The conventional view is that a child who experiences a broken home, or who never has known what it is like to live in a two-parent family, will be at a serious disadvantage compared with children raised in more stable and traditional environments. The child from a broken home will face a far greater risk of stunted personality growth and development. A disrupted familiy life may also cause serious problems in the future.

Several investigators recently have challenged this view, claiming that statistical evidence, fragmentary as it may be, does not fully coincide with these notions. In fact, some analysts even assert that the generally held view about the burden carried by children of divorced parents reflects more traditional morals and mores than empirical evidence.

While the total impact of parental separation upon childhood development remains uncertain, the economic burdens are subject to verification. Even if a child experiences no psychological problems in adjusting to a disrupted household environment, in many cases the family's financial circumstances will be significantly altered, and support for the children may be radically diminished. Child support of youngsters in broken homes has proven to be a difficult problem, and the economic prospects of living in a female-headed household are, on average, much bleaker than those in a husband-wife family.

Child Development

Prior to the recent advances in statistical and computer-aided research, studies of the impact of broken homes on children relied heavily on the case-study approach. Using this methodology in the 1920s, one analyst found a common pattern in many separated families. The initial intellectual acceptance of separation by family members was followed by an emotional or "gut level" period of shock, which hit the children even more seriously than their parents. When normal patterns and habits were disrupted, an increasing sense of bitterness and pain were felt. The adjustment was accompanied by frustration, and many youngsters could not fully accept the changes in their lives for quite a number of years. [14]

This view that divorce itself and living in a one-parent family hinder child development became the predominant judgment, and it became conventional wisdom. However, as data sources expanded and research technology improved, analysts employed newly designed statistical survey methods to examine much larger samples than could be studied under the case-study approach. Using these newer—and presumably better—research methods, analysts tested whether significant statistical differences existed between children from stable two-parent households and those raised in broken homes.

Of course, these computer studies are not without their difficulties. One major problem has to do with data samples. Even sound findings based on properly selected variables may have limited applicability if the data come from only one city or area, which cannot represent the entire American population. It is also very difficult and highly risky to use cross-sectional data—even if they are available annually—to predict what will happen during the course of several years. Furthermore, even the most advanced research models often contain key assumptions that are not tested, so that hidden value judgments may distort the researcher's findings.

Measuring personality characterictics and social relationships involves a high degree of subjectivity, compounding the difficulties faced by the investigator. Moreover, it is hard to model the path of causation and to control for the various factors even if subjective opinions can be held to a minimum. The net results of being raised in a broken home are often difficult to disentangle and separate from such variables as economic and social status. In fact, all these various forces may be highly interrelated in many cases. Also, a good portion of the data fed into computers for these studies came from individual self-assessments of doubtful accuracy. For example, depending upon the circumstances, a child's responses about his or her ability to make and hold onto friends are not only subjective, they may also be intentionally misleading. For similar reasons, a female head of a household might find it very difficult to acknowledge that she believes her children have been damaged because of her divorce or she may attribute her children's deficiencies to the divorce even if their difficulties are not related to that event. In many of the studies researchers have tried to create controls that will reveal some of these self-assessment difficulties.

In brief, finding hard evidence is elusive, and this raises questions about the proper mode of statistical comparison. Ideally, children from broken homes should be compared with children from intact families burdened with parental conflicts. Such a comparison assumes that the investigator can detect families with deep-seated problems as distinguished from "happy" families.

These reservations about the attitudinal and child-development studies notwithstanding, the findings of this statistical research should not be rejected outright. On the whole, the studies tend to paint a picture that is somewhat different from the standard notion. If these investigations are correct, then the net result of a broken home on child development is not as harsh, or necessarily as detrimental, as is often assumed.

Arguing that in the vast majority of cases the causes of a divorce can be found in deep-seated problems such as alcoholism, drug abuse, violence, nonsupport, adultery, and desertion, one study questioned whether these parents, had they remained married, could have provided a better environment for their children than a single-parent household. Though only about one of ten single mothers reported that her children were harder to handle after the divorce, those mothers who experienced a high degree of trauma during the divorce process also reported that their children were the least happy.[15] About half of the divorced women sampled in the study remarried by the 26th month after their divorce. Hence, many children lived only a short time in a one-parent family. Of the remarried mothers, about three-quarters believed that the lives of their children were better in the second marriage than in the first. While more than 80 percent of the divorced mothers indicated that prior to the divorce they seriously feared the separation would harm their children, almost 55 percent reported no increase in child-related problems once the home was split apart.

Another study found a positive relationship between juvenile delinquency and broken homes, even when the economic status of families was considered. The study suggested a strong relationship between juvenile delinquency and broken homes if the single-parent household resulted from the death of a parent rather than a divorce.[16] However, some analysts have questioned these findings. If divorce and delinquency are more apt to happen to children in poorer and lower-social-status households, then other environmental factors may be the real causes of both divorce and delinquency. Also, family disorganization, and not divorce, may be the key factor.[17]

Other studies have tried to compare selected personality characteristics, as measured by standardized tests and interviews, of children raised in broken homes and youngsters living in two-parent families. This body of research has tended to find that several personality characteristics, including health and mental problems, appear to be more related to family social and economic status than to divorce. Researchers have found no evidence of a clear-cut superiority of adolescents raised in two-parent families compared with children who live in broken homes. Some studies have found no statistically significant difference in school grades, attitudes toward school, and participation in school activities. In fact, some researchers have even contended that the "inimical effects" often associated with children from broken homes compared with those from intact families are almost uniformly absent.[18] Investigators have also compared children from broken homes with youngsters raised in unhappy, but intact, families. The results indicate only very small differences in personality measures between the two. Also, children from broken homes have a lower chance of experiencing psychosomatic illnesses than youngsters in unbroken, but unhappy, families.[19]

A good portion of the impact of a broken home may be related to how a child viewed family life prior to the disintegration. One study of college-age youths found that children subjected to constant parental bickering before a divorce adjust more easily to a broken home than did youngsters who were taken by surprise.[20] Other researchers claim that parents' divorce does slightly increase the likelihood that their children also will experience a divorce.[21]

While the majority of studies concerning the impact of broken homes on children have concluded that divorce may not be as detrimental to child development as is often assumed, not all investigations agree with this finding. For example, based on a sample of 18,000 youngsters, a study commissioned by the National Association of Elementary School Principals found that children from broken homes are late to school or miss more days of class more often and are more likely to drop out or be expelled than children residing with both parents. Of all the elementary and secondary school children sampled, 40 percent of those living with one parent were low achievers, compared with 24 percent of those living with a father and mother. At the other end of the scale, 30 percent of the two-parent children were ranked as high achievers compared with 17 percent of single-parent youths.[22] However, it is not clear from this study how much of these differences can be traced to divorce and how much to economic and other social conditions.

Labor economists have examined the impact of family disruptions on youths' ability to remain in school and/or their prospects in the labor market. As might be expected, teenagers living with one parent are more likely to seek and hold a job than classmates living with two parents, regardless of race, family income, the educational attainment of the family head, and family size.[23] A related hypothesis, which was tested, is that having an adult male in the house helps a youth in landing a job. The findings indicated that a youth who lives in a household headed by a female has slightly less chance of finding productive employment than a youngster who lives in a male-headed household.[24]

The body of research concerning the impact on child development of being raised in a broken home suggests that the patterns are highly complex, and the results defy simple conclusions. Nevertheless, Alvin Schorr concluded that most children from single-parent families are just as able to cope with life problems as children raised in husband-wife families.[25] However, having noted this, analysts who deny the debilitating impact of divorce upon children, like the captain of the Titantic, may fail to perceive the approaching of an iceberg.

Child Support

Besides facing difficult psychological adjustments, most children who experience a family disruption will also be forced into reduced economic circumstances. The average family income of households headed by an unmarried female is only about half the size of the average income for all families. Divorce is a significant predictor of shifts in the economic status of women, and the direction is almost always downward in the cases of divorce and separation. This does not hold true for men.

A profile of single household heads shows that they are mostly female; the chances are greater that they are members of a minority group; they are less educated; far less regularly employed; and much more likely to be poor. Roughly a third of the single-parent families have preschool children, and almost two of three one-parent households receive some income from a public assistance program.[26]

The chances are about two in three that a divorced, separated, never married, or remarried mother with a child will not receive child-support payments from the father (figure 11). In 1978 the mean family income of a female household head with children was $6,200 if she received no child support, but it was 44 percent greater if she did get child-support payments.

FIGURE 11.

The chances that a divorced, separated, never-married or remarried mother will receive child-support payments are slim.

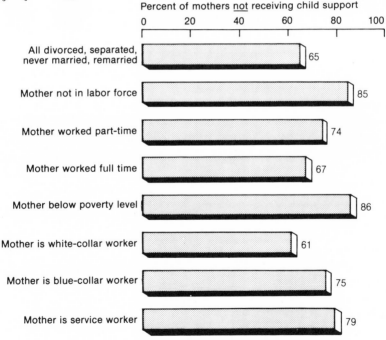

Percent of mothers not receiving child support

All divorced, separated, never married, remarried	65
Mother not in labor force	85
Mother worked part-time	74
Mother worked full time	67
Mother below poverty level	86
Mother is white-collar worker	61
Mother is blue-collar worker	75
Mother is service worker	79

Source: U.S., Department of Commerce, Bureau of the Census

Child-support payments, when they exist, tend to be meager. In 1978, the mean amount paid by fathers not living with their children but contributing to child support was about $1,800 per year.[27] Also, the number of children involved does not significantly affect average payments per family. Child support accounts for more than half of family income in one of five cases receiving such payments, but half of all the women getting child support find that these payments represent less than 20 percent of their total family income. If a woman remarries, then the chances are further reduced that she will receive child-support payments. Separated mothers are far less likely to receive any payments than are divorced mothers, and almost none of the never-married mothers are apt to get any payments.

There is also a clear pattern between child-support payments and the personal characteristics of the unmarried mother. While black women represent 27 percent of all the women eligible for these payments, only 11 percent of the women who receive child support are black. The average payment to a white mother is 44 percent greater than the amount a black mother receives. Also, older women and women with more education tend to receive larger payments. Women who get child-support payments also are more likely to be employed than those who do not.

The father's ability to pay—measured by his earnings the year before the divorce or separation—is a key factor in determining both the chances that payments will be made and their size. Whether the marriage was the man's first also is a factor, because a remarried man tends to pay less. An Urban Institute study found that men with annual earnings of about twice the poverty threshold, and who did make payments, allocated one-eighth of their income to their former families. Men with lower incomes who were contributing to child support were transferring a higher proportion of their before-tax income.[28]

Enforcement of child support has been lax although the responsibility to provide support for children exists by statute or common law in all American jurisdictions. At the time of a divorce or separation a court determines the amount of support, and the awards vary widely between—and even within—jurisdictions. However, the court order is only the first hurdle in what can prove to be a very long and unsuccessful process. Often payments are not made, or they are highly irregular, or less than the awarded amount. The parent with custody of the children can take legal action, but this has been a highly expensive and futile experience in many cases.[29]

Because of the lack of private support payments, public funds have been increasingly used to meet the basic economic needs of broken homes. The Department of Health and Human Services has established an office of child support enforcement, which provides incentives and technical assistance to encourage states and counties to collect more money from absent parents, but enforcement is left to the states unless expenditure of federal funds is involved. If local authorities cannot track down a parent who has failed to make court-ordered child-support payments, then the federal parent locator system—which uses social security and other administrative data—can be brought into the picture. While the numbers involved, both in terms of dollars and missing parents, only scratch the surface of the problem, about $3.33 is collected in child-support payments for every dollar spent on the program.

Family disruption has induced many women to enter the labor force. Given the low educational attainment of many single female parents, and racial and sexual discrimination in the labor market, it should come as no surprise that their earnings often are inadequate to lift their families out of destitution. For many female-headed families, the income garnered from work has proven to be less than a godsend.

The private decisions between two parents on splitting up a home have spilled over to affect the rest of society since private child-support payments have not been enough to mitigate economic hardship for many children who experience family disruptions. Reduced economic circumstances are likely to be one of the most immediate and direct impacts a child from a broken home will experience. For children in husband-wife families, changes in the family income are most closely tied to the labor market experiences of their father in most cases. However, for women the changes in their family income are much less closely tied to their own labor market experiences and hinge more on family composition.[30] Besides emotional trauma, the fact that a father is no longer living in the house can be a major economic blow to the child.

PARENTS AND CHILDREN

Most American children still are raised by two parents and do not experience family disintegration. Yet the traditional picture of childrearing is far less valid now than it has been in the past, and the single-parent family appears to be a permanent and pronounced fixture on the American scene. By contrast, in the past single parents tended to turn their children over to relatives or institutions, and the children would be raised by neither parent. In fact, part of the growth in single-parent families reflects a new determination by unmarried mothers to raise their own children.

The impact of these new forces is hard to quantify or evaluate. The incidence of marital disruption seems to be slightly higher among adults who were affected by divorces in their childhood than by children brought up in stable families. Reduced economic circumstances alone tend to affect the child's probability of continuing in school, and consequently the child's labor market prospects. It is more difficult to form any hard and fast conclusions about the effect of family breakup on children's personality development and their ability to form social relationships. Though some studies indicate that most of the children from broken homes are just as able to cope with the problems of life as children from two-parent families, their conclusions must be regarded as highly tentative because of serious methodological problems.

One major impact of broken homes has been to shift a greater proportion of financial support for children onto public sources. Only a very small minority of single mothers receives any child-support payments, and most often these payments must be supplemented by earnings and government income transfer programs.

These developments pose some of the most serious challenges that the American family system must face. Yet the family as an institution has proven to be highly resilient in the past, and new arrangements are evolving to meet these very tough challenges. American families are not rigid and static institutions, and they are showing ways to cope, adapt, and evolve in this shifting environment.

Chapter Five

THE FAMILY AND WORK GO TOGETHER

> When a girl leaves her home at eighteen, she does one
> of two things. Either she falls into saving hands and
> becomes better, or she rapidly assumes the
> cosmopolitan standard of virtue and becomes worse.
> Theodore Dreiser, *Sister Carrie*

FAMILY WORK ROLES

When Caroline Meeber boarded the train for Chicago
in 1889, with her cheap imitation alligator-skin satchel and purse
containing a grand total of $4, Dreiser tells us that she was "full of
the illusions of ignorance and youth." No husband would be waiting
to love, provide, and protect her. She would have to make her own
way in a cold city, and she would have to enter the rough and tumble
world of the wage earner. Her opportunities in the labor market
would be far inferior to those for most men. She would be relegated
to "women's work," which consisted mostly of positions on the
bottom rungs of the job ladder. The wages would be less than those
earned by men, and the chances for advancement would be slim.
This harsh reality facing her would soon enough erode all of her
youthful illusions.

If she had a choice between falling into saving masculine hands
accompanied by a hearth and home or becoming a working girl, it
was assumed that she would pick the former option, as would any
sane young woman. The presumption was that if a woman had

chosen gainful employment it was because the matrimonial option had failed to materialize or because the unfortunate woman had married a man who was not a good provider.

These views concerning a woman's place in the industrial society were taken as self-evident and were shared by women and men alike. The nuclear family was supposed to symbolize a successful refuge from a rough world, and within the family there was to be rigid division of labor along sexual lines. The husband was the breadwinner, while the woman was the good wife, mother, cook, and housekeeper. If a woman could afford to stay home and not work, then her place was to remain in the house. Whether or not women had been brainwashed into believing this ethos, a vast majority of them espoused these norms in the not too distant past.

The tables have turned almost full circle. With more than half of the adult female population in the labor force, there have been tremendous shifts in societal norms. In fact, wives who are still living with their husbands have represented the vast bulk of new female workers who now labor outside the home. Eli Ginzberg has called this dramatic growth of women seeking gainful employment in the paid labor force "the single most outstanding phenomenon of our century."[1] At one time it was the working woman who was led to believe—through novels, magazines, movies, and a whole host of cultural devices—that she was the oddity. Something was lacking in her life that would only be filled by being a full-time wife and mother. Now these cultural forces have almost reversed, and the woman who does not have a career outside the home is often depicted as the individual whose life lacks fulfillment.

Laboring in the work force and being a wife and mother are not, of course, mutually exclusive. More than half of all wives with spouse present—to borrow Census Bureau language—are trying to live both roles. Today the full-time housewife is viewed by some as almost an endangered species, as more than five out of seven American adults approve of a married woman entering the work force even if her husband is capable of supporting her. Nearly half of all adults indicate that they believe a marriage would be the most satisfying to them if both the husband and wife worked and shared in child care and housework. These attitudinal findings may indicate vast shifts in social roles, but women still face, in part, a double standard. While 90 percent of wives insist that they would be willing to give up their careers if their work conflicted with their husbands' interests, only 22 percent believe that their husbands would be willing to make the same sacrifices for them. Also, while the stigma of being a working wife has vastly diminished, roughly 40 percent of American adults still believe that working women are not as good mothers as women who stay at home all day.[2]

Adding Underpaid to Unpaid Work

An old nursery rhyme may have been true in the past:

Clap hands, clap hands, until Daddy comes home
Because Daddy's got money and Mommy's got none.

But this is currently far from an accurate picture of many American households. Motherhood has become far less of a roadblock to paid employment outside of the home. There is a high probability that the child either will have to clap hands alone, with another relative, or in a day care facility, until both daddy *and* mommy come home. And once both parents are home, daddy is not the only person who has money. This fact raises questions not only about the role of the woman outside the household, but it also challenges her traditional subordinate status within the home, even if the wife does not match the husband's earnings. Indeed, while emphasis is placed on the impact of female employment on the work force, a far more subtle transformation may be taking place inside of the family. Instead of liberation, some women may find that they have become part of the "secretarial proletariat." As one feminist writer put it: "Many working women are married (I was married during my last job; since my husband was sick at the time, I was the sole support of the household, on a salary that was half what my husband could make with the same qualifications). Then we have two full-time jobs instead of just one—underpaid clerical worker and unpaid housekeeper."[3]

Regardless of equity, the old patterns of stereotyped sexual work roles within the family were clear and largely unchallenged. For better or for worse, these traditional arrangements are being replaced by numerous and highly varied life styles. It cannot be expected that family structures will come away untouched, and shifting patterns of work life have had a pronounced impact on the American family. Some fear that these complex forces will erode the family institution and could be one more nail in its coffin.

When a girl now reaches her eighteenth birthday, she usually has far wider choices than those which faced Dreiser's heroine. The opportunity for additional study or education is now open to more women than in previous generations. Today more women are enrolled in college than men, and other women enroll in vocational training and other institutions that prepare them for career development. The rewards of work have attracted a growing number of young women, and their resulting economic independence permits postponement of marriage.

By contrast, in the past the job was more of a way station than a permanent decision—an experience to be had before falling into saving hands. At one time female work life patterns followed an "M" curve. Women's labor force participation reached a peak in their early twenties, and then fell as they withdrew from paid employment to get married, and have children, while depending on the husband for support. As the children grew up, some women would reenter the labor force. This trend formed the second peak on the "M" curve. All in all, this female labor force pattern was quite different from the one displayed by men, most of whom continued to work well past midlife.

Women's work life patterns are changing, moving closer to men's (figure 12). This could have a major impact on the family. As more young women have sought the challenges of the labor market, they have tended to postpone marriage. While women have a long way to go before they achieve equality with men in the work force, a growing number of women, aided by Uncle Sam's pressures, have found employment on higher rungs of the job ladder.

Some suggest that women who achieve improved earnings potential and higher job status may tend to reject marriage as they will not need a man to provide for them. This speculation has obvious flaws. By developing their own careers women might opt for different life styles. But rejection of vicarious living, through a husband's career and children, should not be equated with repudiating marriage. Men have been economically independent for years, yet they have clung to the institution of marriage and have been willing to support it. This does not negate the probability that the entry of married women into the work force could affect the family if it proved to increase the divorce rate. In the past a wife may have stayed in a bad marriage because opportunities for entering the labor force and making it on her own were limited. Financial insecurity and dependence on the part of the woman, and not love, may have been the binding glue that has held many a marriage together. As a woman experiences or believes that she can earn her own way in the world, shifting work roles could prove to be an added incentive to break up a family.

The massive entry of mothers into the work force has intensified concerns whether a working mother can be as good a parent to her children as a full-time housewife. If the mother is not at home for

FIGURE 12.

While differences persist, the
age patterns of women in the labor force
are moving closer to those of men.

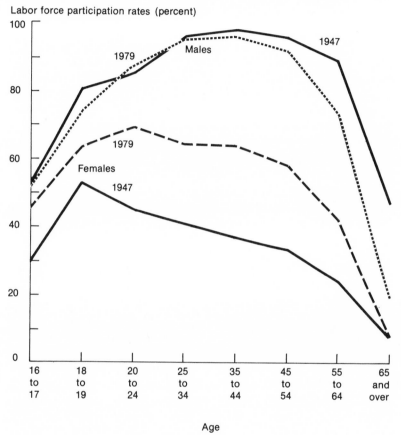

Labor force participation rates (percent)

Source: U.S., Department of Labor, Bureau of Labor Statistics

a good portion of the day, the availability of suitable child care
becomes a major problem. Aside from the emotional concerns over
adjustments to new child care arrangements, the economic costs
cannot be ignored. Good institutional child care is costly and society
is moving slowly in funding such facilities. As the number of chil-

dren in public schools declines, part of the "savings" are being allocated to the care and education of younger children. "Free" schooling for 5-year-olds is becoming universal and facilities for 4-year-olds and even younger children are expanding. Still, provision of child care is a highly sensitive issue, and it will remain an intense emotional consideration for many years to come.

A second problem faced by women who find themselves wage earners yet still responsible for the vast majority of the housework is the reallocation of work roles within the family. As women behave more like men in the labor force, men will have to learn to readjust their roles in the home. More than reallocations of cooking, cleaning, shopping, and childrearing responsibilities are involved; there is a need to reexamine traditional power relationships within the family. Some mistakenly confuse sexually stereotyped work roles with the real essence of what it means to be part of a family. Shifting work responsibilities have a good deal of evolutionary potential for the family, and they can have many positive impacts on home life. When matters concerning the household exchequer are dealt with, a mother is much less likely to just shrug her shoulders and lament that "father knows best" if she has had a major role in filling the family's coffers. A family with two wage earners may be expected to have a far different pattern of sharing responsibilities than the traditional one-earner household.

Ethos and Reality

The old ethos concerning a woman's place in the home is more a creation of Victorian ideology than a description of historic reality. Any future predictions about women in the labor force should consider the various economic, social, and political factors that have led to the major upsurge in female labor force participation rates. While the vast numbers of women entering the work force may have transformed the family and society, it is still a long way from being a glorious revolution for most females. Job discrimination, occupational segregation, lower wages, and limited room for advancement still face all too many female workers.

To assert that a woman's place was in the home while the man's natural habitat was the factory or office contained some elements of fact in latter stages of industrial society. When agriculture was the prime source of employment for the vast majority of the popu-lation, a man's place was not that far removed from the home, and the wife was beside him sharing in homestead chores. However, in addition to cooking, cleaning, and caring for children, wives also provided the needed labor for spinning, weaving, making soap, shoes, candles, and many of the other essentials consumed by the household. While many jobs were allocated on the basis of sex, there was no question that women worked very hard—often right along with the men—in this agrarian economy.[4] Under these conditions, women's work was vital to the survival of the family. Very few women have ever belonged to a leisure class that had no work responsibilities, toil, or obligations in the production process.

What has changed is not the fact of women's work, but the institutional arrangements, occupations, and settings in which they work. Even under current labor force definitions, a person is counted in the work force if the individual works without pay for 15 hours or more a week for a family business.

The industrial revolution separated the work place from the home. During the colonial period, spinning and weaving were household chores done by women and children. Most of this country's early factories produced textiles, and instead of spinning and weaving in the home many women did these jobs in factories. Because of a rapidly growing economy, a vast supply of unsettled land, and frequent shortages of labor, employers sought women for certain types of jobs. They also welcomed women as a cheaper source of labor than men. A good number of the hands that performed the work on the new machines belonged to women.[5] In fact, using women as a source of labor was in some ways encouraged by the government. Alexander Hamilton insisted that one of the chief benefits of promoting industrialization was that it would raise the living standards of the masses. He noted: "It is worthy of particular remark, that in general, women . . . are rendered more useful by manufacturing establishments than they would otherwise be. . . . The rise of manufacturers has elevated the females belonging to the families of the cultivators of the soil from a state of penury . . . to competence and industry."[6]

Lacking historical perspective, one could easily believe that conflict over a woman's place in society is only a modern phenomenon. But even a cursory examination of social history discloses that past generations and families were racked by the same tensions. It took a concerted effort from the pulpit and other social agencies—reinforced by novelists and newspaper scribes—to persuade women that they had a divinely ordained task to play the role of supporting actress to their husbands, and to create a haven for them from the outside world. Unmarried women were regarded as pitiable encumbrances, as females had a biological destiny that they were forbidden to fulfill without marriage vows. A long list of nineteenth-century educators, theologians, and political leaders could be cited who espoused these views. Even in the 1930s, anthropologist Margaret Mead asserted that a woman had the choice of either becoming an achieving individual and less of a woman, or she could be a woman and "therefore less of an achieving individual." As recently as 1955, Adlai Stevenson told the Smith College graduating class that their primary task was to "influence man and boy" through the "humble role of housewife."[7]

Yet the economy often required the labor of women to fill shortages, and many women always desired to establish careers outside the home. The resolution of these conflicting forces created a double standard for women entering or wishing to enter gainful employment. Several different factors may have contributed to the intensification of the notion during the height of the Victorian era that a woman should confine her work to the home. The gradual diminution of unsettled land reduced one major escape valve for urban male workers; relatively more men had to seek employment in industrialized urban centers. Also, the influx of immigrants swelled the labor supply. As a result, the solution to public concern over the specter of male unemployment was resolved by banning women from the labor market.[8]

Other observers stressed fertility factors. Theodore Roosevelt saw ominous warnings in the fertility trends at the turn of the century. The upper crust of society, or, as he put it, "the highest races," were vastly reducing the number of children they brought into the world, while the lower orders continued multiplying. Roosevelt and others

The Work Ethic

felt that the "better people" ought to have more children and that a woman in this category who was so "selfish" that she should not reduce her activities outside the home was nothing more than "a criminal against the race."[9]

Researchers have tried to place this change in attitudes toward working women in a larger social context. As romantic love replaced arranged marriages, the goals of marriage and the family were elevated. Domesticity was expected to provide spiritual bliss. Victorians saw the family, to use Ruskin's words, as "a sacred place; a temple of the hearth."[10] Also, notions concerning childhood changed. Focusing on the highly structured bourgeois family system, Christopher Lasch has suggested that industrialization of the production process required an "industrialization in reproduction." Children were recognized as persons with distinctive attributes, making childrearing more demanding, and Lasch claims the "bourgeois family simultaneously degraded and exalted women." Specialization of work roles within the family haven became more detailed and segregated along sexual lines. Childbearing and rearing came to be viewed as a full-time occupation for married women who belonged to the bourgeoisie. Along with private property, the rise of the nuclear family was to provide a refuge from a rough competitive world, and a wife's main role came to be the custodian of this haven. The division of labor that took place in the marketplace was mirrored within the family. According to Lasch, the zenith of laissez-faire capitalism during the late Victorian era required that society strengthen its mores concerning a woman's place in the home.[11]

Whether any, or all, of these theories can explain female labor force participation patterns toward the end of the 1800s remains a matter of taste, but there is little dispute about the facts. A dual standard for women was in full force by the end of the Victorian era in America. Unmarried women outside the upper circles of society might be encouraged to enter the work force for a time, but the goal was still to have them marry and bear children. Two types of married women might work outside of the home without society's disapproval—black women (most of whom lived and labored in the South) and immigrant women (who worked in Northeastern industrial centers).

By 1890, fewer than one of five women age 14 years and over were in the labor force. The vast majority of these workers were single; married women living with their husbands accounted for only 14 percent of the working women. Even widowed and divorced women showed a much lower propensity to enter the work force than single women. More than a third of single women were in the labor force, but 19 of 20 married women stayed at home and did not seek paid employment.[12]

A study conducted during this era found that three of four female workers were immigrants. A black woman faced far different economic and social conditions from the rest of the female population. Because the chances were far greater that black men could not earn enough to keep their families out of destitution, black wives were obliged to enter the labor force in greater relative numbers than white wives. About 4 percent of white wives sought employment, but about 25 percent of black wives were in the labor force during this period. Black widows faced even harsher economic realities, and more than two-thirds of them became wage earners.[13] Most of the black women who worked were either field hands or domestic servants. These working women—blacks and immigrants—were not expected to adhere to the norm concerning a woman's place; they were not part of the middle class.

While wives were subordinate to their husbands, an agrarian economy blurred the sharp work distinction between spouses. The realities of farming created an internal labor market within the household where chores were allocated and products were exchanged and consumed. There was no question that both the husband and wife worked to provide the means of household subsistence. When the work location was removed from the home, the movement of women into the labor force started to rise.

As paid employment was not a socially acceptable option, middle-class women found respectable alternate exits from home. Various volunteer causes, not all in the genteel tradition—for example, the suffragette movement—attracted the interests and occupied the time of many women. Apart from earnings, there is often not much difference between the work done by volunteers and that done on paid jobs, and many unpaid workers perform tasks that have a direct equivalent in the paid work force. A national commission concluded in 1979 that distinguishing between work that is paid and work that is not can be "a somewhat arbitrary practice."[14]

Women played a major role in the social and legislative campaigns of the pre–World War I Progressive era. Also, many of the liberal reforms of this period were directed toward improving the working conditions of women. Coming from the "upper crust," Bessie Van Vorst and her sister-in-law, Marie Van Vorst, were prevented by prevailing custom from becoming wage earners, but this did not stop them from dressing as factory girls and exploring the conditions of female employment. The results of their direct observations (published in 1903 as *The Woman Who Toils*) aroused the country to the lot of female factory workers. A minimum wage for women and children, as well as laws covering the maximum number of hours they could work, were high on the agenda of reformers. Middle-class groups, such as the National Consumers League, were often the prime forces fighting for these laws, and married women played a major role in these reform movements.[15]

The concern that the family is being besieged is not new. The ethos and reality displayed a good deal of tension even when only a few married women dared to become paid workers. Many wives cast in the full-time role of mother and housewife were not willing to remain in the home all day. Numerous other outlets attracted a good deal of their attention besides the family. During the early part of this century many male observers were struck by tensions created by the changing status of women. Alarmed by the changes, the popular press, as well as some learned journals, were quick to predict the demise of the family.

At one time it may have been the norm to envision a domestic joy created by a wife who only labored in the home. However, even back then there was a realization that it might be "an illusory center, or perhaps not a center at all." A Hedda Gabler or an Emma Bovary wanted, and reached out for, something more than this norm. They were not alone. Other less known commentators preached the same theme, "no matter how committed they were to the contemporary middle-class orthodoxies."[16]

Ours is not the first era that has experienced the anxieties caused by a changing status of women. Family work roles have not remained static, and they always have had to adapt to and accommodate shifting economic and social conditions. The world in which the bulk of the labor force was devoted to the production of goods is fading, just as did the world in which agriculture dominated the economic scene. The shift from manufacturing to service and information-processing activities is bound to have an impact on the family. New norms concerning family work roles are evolving. However, as indicated by historical changes in work roles, the family has shown a remarkable ability to survive and adjust to new realities. There are many different patterns of work roles under which the family can flourish, and those who equate the institution with the pattern that reached its ascendancy during the late Victorian era reflect their biases, or ignorance, of the past.

FIGURE 13.

The vast increase of women in the work force has occurred during recent decades.

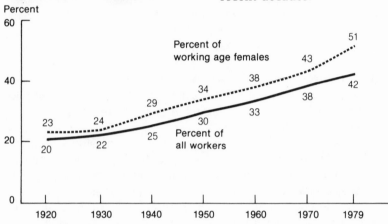

Percent

Percent of working age females

Percent of all workers

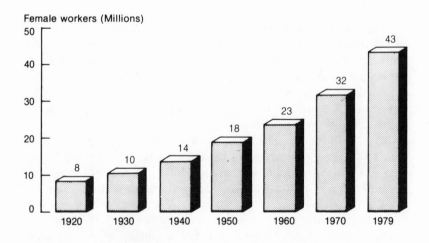

Female workers (Millions)

Source: U.S., Department of Labor, Bureau of Labor Statistics

WOMEN AT WORK

Between the early part of this century and World War II the role of women in society may have changed, but women did not rush into the labor force. Sociologists displayed a voracious appetite for investigating the family, carefully centering their attention on social and economic variables that might lead to a stable marriage, safe subjects even for Victorian social scientists. Alternative life styles and family work patterns remained, however, outside the pale. The idea that the husband would be the sole provider in a family and the wife would not be in the labor force was usually assumed as a given.

Cultural biases aside, the issues studied by the social scientists reflected the stability of family structure and the lack of change during the first four decades of this century in the tasks performed by women. Their participation in the labor force registered little change during this period, and the dual standard as to the types of women who could seek paid employment remained in effect (figure 13). Their occupational pattern also remained almost constant. In 1920 approximately 12 percent of the women at work were in professional jobs, the same percentage as two decades later. Nearly three of four professional women were elementary school teachers or nurses. As typing and stenography expanded, these occupations became women's work, and by 1930 one-third of the female labor force was employed in clerical occupations.

Restrictions on female paid employment were in line with social norms, but sometimes these norms became institutionalized in laws. The Social Security Act of 1935—the cornerstone of the welfare state—established what later became Aid to Families with Dependent Children (AFDC). Destitute and husbandless mothers were entitled to receive support payments, and these mothers were not expected to work, reflecting not only the dearth of jobs during the 1930s but also the belief that a mother's place was in the home with her children. Some of the problems that have beset AFDC in recent years stem from a shift in this belief, and many policymakers now think that some welfare mothers should work. The structure of other social security payments and the tax system often favors the older family work pattern; for example, federal income tax rules favor families in which only one spouse works. These conditions reflect not only sexual bias, but also the comparative recency of the upsurge of women in the labor force. Often formal institutional arrangements lag behind significant changes in social conditions.

World War II—A Launching Pad

World War II stands as a major break in female work patterns. The war effort's high demands for labor, and patriotic fervor induced many women to join the labor force boosting the size of the female work force by 57 percent during the war. Beyond the unprecedented numbers, women entered numerous occupations that were previously the exclusive domain of men. "Rosie the Riveter" became a folk heroine. Gainful employment was sought not only by single and minority women, but also by married women. This massive dose of work experience persuaded many women to remain in the labor force after the war. The influx of women into the work force has continued ever since.

Wives and mothers have played a key role in the changing composition of the labor force in recent decades. The number of working mothers has more than quadrupled since World War II, while the total number of female workers has more than doubled. By 1980, about 17 million mothers with children under 18 were working or seeking work, accounting for 55 percent of the mothers with children that age—compared with 30 percent two decades earlier, and less than ten percent in 1940. Since the end of World War II, women, mostly married, accounted for about three-fifths of the total increase in civilian employment. American women of all classes and backgrounds have entered the labor market. More than half of all married women are now employed. In 1980, 24 million working wives comprised close to one-fourth of the entire labor force.

Several factors stand out in any analysis explaining the rise in female labor force participation. Medical technology made it possible to determine the number and spacing of children while improvements in home technology have facilitated household maintenance. This has reduced the amount of time required to carry out the woman's traditional role of running a household and raising children, and it has given women more time to devote to other activities including employment outside the home. As more women obtained longer doses of education and higher paying jobs, their opportunity costs of not working rose. Social and cultural factors have also played a role as the stigma once associated with wives' working has vastly diminished and concepts regarding the father's participation in childrearing are being changed, albeit rather slowly.

Money also played a role in attracting women to the labor market. While discrimination based on sex remains a powerful force in the work place, women's groups backed by civil rights laws insisted on opening better paying "men's" jobs to women, and employers changed many time-honored practices. Opportunities for higher pay and status have induced more women to seek work outside the home.

After World War II, some analysts predicted that family work patterns would return to the older norm. They reasoned that rising productivity and economic growth would continue to boost the income earned by husbands, thus reducing the need for another check and inducing wives to return to their homes. This, of course, did not happen, as economists failed to consider the nonpecuniary attractions of work and the appetite for more income. Not discouraged by one failure to predict women's behavior, economists turned to new models that would explain the labor market behavior of married women.[17]

The newer economic theories focus on the entire household instead of just on the individual. They assume that the decisions to enter the labor force, and the number of hours that are worked, depend on many variables affecting family life. The supply of labor is treated as a joint household or family decision.[18] For example, as a husband's income rises, his family will be able to purchase more timesaving household goods, which will reduce the number of hours required to keep up a home and give the wife more time to work outside the home.

Since World War II American households have shown a strong propensity to increase their consumption of goods and services. Many wives joined the work force to finance these upward consumption patterns. Like the mechanical rabbit leading the greyhounds around the racetrack, these aspirations have consistently stayed ahead of productivity, often requiring another pay check in the chase for the "good life." In the inflationary 1970s and early 1980s another check became necessary just to maintain the standard of living to which the families had become accustomed. By 1980, three of five husband-wife families had at least two household members in the labor force; in most cases, the husband and the wife.

Many working wives make a significant contribution to the income of a household. Wives employed year-round, full time earn about 38 percent of their families' total income. The median family income for two-earner couples is more than 30 percent higher than for those where only the husband works. During the 1970s, the number of children in husband-wife families declined by more than 9 million. Nevertheless, the number of children whose mothers work rose by almost 2 million. As a result, almost half of all children in husband-wife families now have working mothers—up from 38 percent in 1970.

Reductions in family size have also helped women enter the labor force, although the direction of causation is difficult to fix. One might say that women first decided to have fewer children, and this decision led them to seek employment outside the home. Conversely, it could be argued that women first decided to enter the labor force, and this decision led them to have fewer children. Obviating the need to enter into a chicken-and-egg controversy, it appears that both forces have symbiotically worked to reinforce these family and labor market trends.

In addition, a growing number of women are heading households. Most of these women must work out of economic necessity. Divorced, separated, and widowed women have accounted for about 11 percent of the expansion in the work force since 1950. About three-fourths of divorcees now work, but less than one-fourth of widows are in the labor force. The latter are generally older, and many receive public or private pensions.

About 60 percent of female-headed families include minor children. These female heads rear almost 12 million children, and they provide for an additional 5.5 million persons in their households. Close to 29 percent of female family heads are widows, over 50 percent are divorced or separated, and close to 16 percent are single women who have never married—although three-fifths of them have had children.[19] The growth in female-headed households has been a strong force leading to the increase in the number of women who enter the labor force.

Educational attainment is more a determinant of labor force participation for women than it is for men, who, once out of school, tend to stay in the labor force regardless of educational attainment. By the close of the 1970s the participation rate ranged from 26 percent for women with an elementary education to 66 percent for women with a college education. Also, the job opportunities for college-educated women have increased substantially. Better-educated women are able to take advantage of the rising demand in the expanding professional and technical occupations. Though the number of professional women is still small, women have made some significant gains in these fields. Women who have invested in a college education—and graduate studies—may also be more reluctant to forego the rewards from work in professional fields because their opportunity costs of staying at home are greater than for less educated women. Women with four or more years of college and who work full time, year-round have incomes that are about twice as much as females with only a grade school education.

While the economic factors behind the increase of women in the labor force may be easier to capture in computer models, many strong cultural forces have played a key role in these changes. The women's liberation movement has had a major impact on heightening the career aspirations of women. Movies, TV, novels, and other media in recent years have often depicted the joys and problems of working women. The net result of these various cultural forces has been to increase the social acceptability—or even inevitability—of women in the work force.

Working Conditions

Working outside the home no longer carries a social stigma for women; indeed, it is considered an honorable pursuit, even for mothers with young children. The unprecedented influx of women into labor markets and the working conditions they experience have affected family life. Suppose a wife with a working husband and only a high school education takes a part-time job as a semiskilled worker. If her remuneration is low, her earnings may be only a marginal addition—though in many cases sorely needed—to the family's budget.

While women have made some inroads into occupations with higher status and earnings, at least in entry-level jobs, the majority still holds jobs in traditionally female occupations with low pay and limited career opportunities. Though women now constitute about one-tenth of all lawyers, judges, doctors, and industrial engineers, most of their employment growth has concentrated in clerical and service occupations. By the end of the 1970s, roughly 80 percent of all clerical workers and 62 percent of all service workers were

TABLE 1. Despite some gains, women workers remain highly concentrated in a few areas of the labor force.

Occupational group	Percent of female employment		Percent of total employment	
	1979	1940	1979	1940
Total				
Number (thousands)	40,446	11,920	—	—
Percent	100	100	41.7	25.9
White-collar workers				
Professional, technical workers	16.1	13.2	43.3	45.4
Managers, officials, proprietors	6.5	3.8	24.6	11.7
Clerical workers	35.0	21.2	80.3	52.6
Salesworkers	6.9	7.0	45.1	27.9
Blue-collar workers				
Craftworkers, foremen	1.8	0.9	5.7	2.1
Operatives	11.5	18.4	32.0	25.7
Nonfarm laborers	1.3	0.8	11.3	3.2
Service workers				
Private household workers	2.6	17.6	97.6	93.8
Service workers (except private household)	17.2	11.3	59.2	40.1
Farm workers	1.2	5.8	18.0	8.0

Source: U.S., Department of Labor, Bureau of Labor Statistics

women, compared with 62 percent and 45 percent, respectively, in 1950 (table 1). About 40 percent of all working women are employed in ten traditional female fields. Male employment shows far less concentration, and less than 10 percent of all male workers are in the ten largest occupations for men.

The concentration of women in a few occupations makes possible a subtle form of discrimination. It reduces the opportunities for advancement, and it also tends to provide employers with an excess supply of female workers for specific job slots. This factor exerts a strong downward pressure on wages for many female occupations. The objective laws of supply and demand—once the female concentration factor is considered—do the rest in keeping down wages for "women's work." The unseen hand does the dirty work, and personnel directors can blame low women's wages on the "system."

*"We have thousands of opportunities for women
with college education. . .if you want to be a secretary."*

A more overt type of discrimination, although equally difficult to
prove, is the presumably objective classification of "women's" occupations under job evaluation systems, which frequently tend to
underestimate the true complexity and responsibility of the jobs
done by women.

While some analysts argue that these conditions are forced on
women by external economic factors, it appears that women's occupational choices also are affected greatly by the socialization process as they grow up. When youngsters are asked "What do you want
to be when you grow up?" most girls choose far fewer occupations
than boys. Through schooling and other cultural forces, young
women often are shunted out of certain fields that are traditionally
held by men. High school mathematics can be one such screening
device in the job market. Survey data from a recent freshman class
at a major American university are illustrative. While 57 percent of
the male freshmen had taken four years of high school math, only
8 percent of their female counterparts had done so. The limited math
restricted women to college careers in the humanities, education,
social welfare, and some social sciences, foreclosing majoring in
other fields of specialization.[20]

Whether or not occupational segregation is used as a discriminatory mechanism, it blocks women from moving up into higher
positions. A typical example is classifying positions requiring similar
or identical qualifications. While the only requirement for both

"claims adjusters" and "claims representatives" in an insurance company may be a college degree, men have been placed as adjusters and women have been hired as representatives. Not only is the starting salary higher for adjusters, but these positions—unlike that of the representatives—are tied into a promotion system leading to better jobs.[21] Government policy has tried to counteract sexual discrimination in the labor force. The Equal Pay Act of 1963 and Title VII of the Civil Rights Act of 1964 prohibit discrimination in employment based on sex as well as on race, color, religion, and national origin. In addition, Executive Order 11246 bans similar discrimination by federal contractors and subcontractors. The 1972 Equal Opportunity Act gave the Equal Employment Opportunity Commission the authority to sue private companies for job discrimination.

The mere passage of legislation, of course, does not guarantee equal employment and earning opportunities. In 1955 the median annual wage for women who worked full time, year-round was 64 percent of men's earnings, compared with 59 percent a generation later. These data must be used with caution; factors other than sex may account for the earnings differentials. For example, female full-time workers tend to labor fewer hours than male full-time workers. However, even after standardization, there is a statistically significant difference between the wages paid for men and women in the same occupational groups. The actual ratios and ratios adjusted for differences in hours worked showed the following pattern of female earnings to male earnings in 1978 for full-time, year-round workers:[22]

Occupational group	Actual ratio	Adjusted ratio
Total	59.4	67.2
Professional and technical workers	64.1	70.2
Managers, officials, and proprietors	54.4	59.8
Clerical workers	59.9	63.9
Salesworkers	45.4	50.7
Skilled and kindred workers	60.8	63.6
Operatives	58.6	64.3
Service workers, excluding private household	63.3	68.3

What is true for occupational groups also holds for specific occupations. Based on a national sample, the median weekly earnings for full-time workers in 1978 showed the following sexual differentials in these occupations:[23]

Occupation	Women	Men	Percent difference
Noncollege teachers	$246	$286	16
Health service workers	145	181	25
Typists, secretaries, and stenographers	170	219	29
Cleaning persons	124	171	38
Waitresses and waiters	113	147	30
Professional health workers (excluding doctors and dentists)	242	265	10

These earnings comparisons give some idea of the wage disparity between men and women, but they do not present a prima facie case of discrimination. For example, many women do not have as strong an attachment to the labor force as men, and females often demonstrate higher turnover and quit rates than males working at similar types of jobs. Also, because of different expectations about future prospects in the labor force, some women do not make as great an investment in education and skill training as men. Economists have tried to determine whether these various differences in work patterns and human capital investments can explain part of the gap between the earnings of men and women. When the data are adjusted to take into consideration these various factors, the earnings gap between men and women narrows. However, there still exists a statistically significant difference that cannot be explained by any of these forces. Sexual occupational segregation and earnings differentials are not, of course, isolated from each other. The chances are that the forces counteracting occupational segregation along sexual lines will be

"Dorothy's a wonderful wife. . .she earns $30,000 a year!"

slow, and a significant earnings differential between men and women will persist for some time.[24]

Also, while the earnings of wives have made an important contribution to household income, only in a few cases has this contribution been close to, or greater than, a husband's earnings. In only about one of six married couples are the wife's earnings comparable to, or more than, those of her husband.[25] If prevailing loose labor markets continue in the 1980s, effective corrective measures will be difficult to achieve in the near future.

Women's entry into the work force outside the home has been described as a subtle revolution, but it has been far from a victorious revolution for many females, if their pay and occupations are taken as an index of success. The goals of equality and equity in the job market are still a long way from becoming a reality.

THE EFFECTS ON FAMILIES

Rising divorce rates and the increase of women's participation in the work force have major effects on the family. Of primary concern are the impacts that the economic independence of women will have for rearing children and marriage decisions. Too frequently changing work roles are construed as causing deterioration of family life in America.

Work and Marriage

In their more imaginative or possibly scary predictions, some futurologists have assumed that the vast upsurge of women in the work force may portend a rejection of marriage. Many women, according to this hypothesis, would rather work than marry. This "independence effect" would reduce the probability that women would marry as they are better able to support themselves. The converse of this concern is that the prospects of becoming a multi–pay check household could encourage marriages. It takes a certain amount of financial security before most men and women are willing to tie the knot. Ample data show that economic downturns tend to postpone marriage because the parties cannot afford to establish a family or are concerned about rainy days ahead. As the economy rebounds and prospects improve for employment, financial security, and advancement, the number of marriages also rises. In the past, only the man's earnings and financial prospects counted in this part of the marriage decision. Now, however, a woman's earning ability can make her more attractive as a marriage partner—a modern version of the old-fashioned dowry.

The trick is to quantify these common sense but conflicting hypotheses associated with working women and marriage in order to reach some judgments about their net effect. As usual, the data are inconclusive and the researchers need to make giant leaps to reach "definite" conclusions on the subject. The above forces often interact and sometimes cancel out each other.[26]

Coincidentally with the increase in women working outside the home, the divorce rate has also increased. Yet, it may be wrong to jump to any simple cause-and-effect conclusions. Just as it may be argued that married women are more prone to seek a divorce if they work, other scenarios also can be offered to explain these data. Perhaps more married women believe that their marriages may end and decide to prepare themselves for the prospects of heading a household. Or, foreseeing many more child-free years, they may want to start a career even before their youngsters grow up and leave home. This would induce seeking employment outside the home even if the marriage stayed intact.

The impact of wives' work upon divorce is no less cloudy than its impact on marriage decisions. An "independence effect"—the realization that she can be a good provider—may increase the chances that a working wife will choose divorce over an unsatisfactory marriage. But the reverse is equally plausible. Tensions grounded in financial problems often play a key role in ending a marriage. Given high unemployment, inflationary problems, and slow growth in real earnings, a working wife can increase household income and relieve some of these pressing financial burdens. By raising a family's standard of living, a working wife may bolster her family's financial and emotional stability.

Psychological factors also should be considered. For example, a wife blocked from a career outside the home may feel caged or shackled to the house—a situation some have dramatically likened to a pressure cooker with no safety valve to release the steam. She may view her only choice as seeking a divorce. On the other hand, if she can find fulfillment through work outside the home, work and marriage can go together to create a stronger and more stable marriage.

Given these conflicting and diverse factors that may have bearing on divorce, statistical demonstration showing direct positive relationship between the two is unattainable. Often studies have reached the conclusion that families in which the wife is working are no more likely to separate or divorce than households in which only the husband is in the labor force.[27]

The relationship between the expanding female work force and reduced fertility rates appears to be clearer. With advances in family planning, a majority of wives have managed to combine motherhood with work. The entry of women into the work force has not led to a vast increase in childlessness among married couples, but, instead, to a lower fertility rate than that among nonworking mothers, when other social and economic factors are taken into consideration. Yet some reservation may be appropriate. In Germany, for example, fertility rates of the native population during the 1970s have declined even more than in the United States, but with no increase in female labor force participation.

The wife's responsibilities outside the home have not filtered back into a major reallocation of responsibilities within the family. With the rising costs of household help, the option to pay another person to do the housework is beyond the means of the vast majority. Also, there are limits as to the chores that can be passed on to the friendly neighborhood supermarket clerk or appliance seller. Even more than in the office or factory, too many household chores cannot be mechanized. Worksharing by other members of the family remains largely a hope. The working wife and mother is, therefore, left to her own devices to cope as wage or salary earner and unpaid houseworker.

When the number of hours a working wife labors outside the home are added to the time spent on household chores, some studies have concluded that most working wives wind up laboring more hours per week than their husbands. Rough estimates based on data from the late 1960s and early 1970s indicated that a wife may average 65 hours on her combined jobs inside and outside the home (assuming that she holds a full-time job in the labor market). This exceeded the average time husbands spent working on the job and in the home by about eight hours per week. However, a more recent study based on data from the mid-1970s indicates that married women labored about the same total hours in their combined jobs as did men—roughly 60 per week. There has been only a very small increase in the hours of housework done by married men (still under three hours per week, or one-sixth the time spent by working wives).[28] It is difficult to make accurate estimates of time use by men and women, but it appears that there still exists a significant sexual division of labor even if total hours worked may be becoming equal for many married men and women.

Just as pathologies within labor markets—such as sexual discrimination—have been slow in changing, so will home adjustments to the new realities of both husband and wife working outside. For example, while most men are just starting to become involved in household responsibilities, this trend soon may be the single largest impact on families associated with wives entering the labor force. In the absence of social upheavals, the slow evolution is toward family work roles based more on equality and less on sexual stereotypes. Many working wives appear to be assuming a larger role in making major family-related decisions than nonworking wives with no earnings, but again, change has been slow. Yet there seem to have been some changes in sharing responsibility and authority.[29]

Child Care

As the number of working mothers with young children rises, child care facilities become increasingly important. However, the types and quality of child care used by working mothers vary widely, with formal child care centers accounting for only a small proportion of day care. Most child care arrangements have remained informal and in the child's or caretaker's home. Licensed child care centers, serving primarily 3- to 5-year-olds, almost quadrupled during the 1960s and 1970s, but they still handle only one of eight children in this age group with working mothers, because the increase in the number of working mothers has outpaced that in the number of child care centers.[30]

Proposals to expand child care services are high on the agenda of most feminist groups. They contend that the lack of child care facilities blocks many women from entering the labor force and that more working mothers would use formal child care institutions if they were subsidized facilities. But costs are a problem, because federal regulations require higher quality and more formal arrangements than those obtained by most working mothers. Enforcement is lax; but if the regulations were met, costs of day care would rise or the number of participating children would be sharply reduced. Although cost estimates for alternative forms of child care are necessarily based on untested assumptions and are therefore questionable, using formal child care facilities is significantly more expensive than having a relative provide child care in one's own home or entrusting the child's care to a relative or a neighbor. Besides cost considerations and preferences for informal as opposed to institutional arrangements, the locations of the facilities and their hours of service are also prime factors in parents' choice whether to place their child in a day care facility or to choose another alternative.

A surprising number of working parents have work schedules that enable them to take care of their children without outside help. In almost one-quarter of the families, the parents work different shifts (or staggered shifts) and, with the help of an older sibling in some cases, they do not need outside child care arrangements. But latchkey cases still abound, where children are left to their own devices after school hours until a parent returns from work. If the labor force trends of mothers continue to follow their recent patterns, the demand for child care services will continue to increase beyond the projected supply.

Many Americans still subscribe to part of the older methods concerning a woman's place; namely, the notion that the well-being of children inevitably suffers when their mothers work outside the home. Though feminists may bristle at such views, protesting that society does not ask whether working men make good fathers, the old beliefs still may determine public policy. Possibly the most significant blow to the expansion of child care was delivered by former President Nixon. In vetoing a bill providing for expansion of federal funds for child care, he cited the potential harm of child care to the fabric of family life as one objection.[31]

The evidence does not indicate, however, that the children of working mothers are worse off because they are entrusted to the care of others. Studies do indicate that working mothers spend less time on child care than women not in the labor force, but not much less. Furthermore, indications are that many working mothers make up for this lost time with quality care by earmarking time to pay exclusive attention to their children. If a mother's employment does not reflect other family problems, it typically does not significantly affect the child's development.[32]

NO GOING BACK

If the survival of the family depends upon women returning to the home to become full-time housewives and mothers, the institution's future existence is indeed fragile. There has been no decline in the career aspirations of women, and continued progress in family planning and household management will let more women become both wives and mothers as well as workers outside of the home. As the potential rewards and work opportunities for women expand, the psychic and economic attractions in the marketplace are likely to exert even greater pull. The occupational choices and prospects for advancement up the job ladder should be expanding. Coupled with this are the increasing number of positions within service industries. Unlike jobs in the goods producing sector of the economy, service industry jobs tend to be more flexible in meeting the particular needs of many women, including part-time employment and flexible work schedules.[33] The growth of the service sector should make it easier for more women to function as workers both inside and outside the home.

With inflationary pressures and slow growth in productivity—leading to sluggish gains and even occasional declines in real earnings—more families will depend on two wage earners just to make ends meet or to finance their growing consumption expectations. Women in the work force, including the majority of married women,

are in the labor force to stay, and this is not a new phenomenon. The "virtuous woman" of the Bible worked and labored very hard. This model of virtue "seeketh wool, and flax and worketh willingly with her hands." And she is "like a merchant's ships; she bringeth her food from afar. . . . She considereth a field, and buyeth it; with the fruit of her hand she planteth a vineyard." And what about her husband? The Good Book tells us that he "is known in the gates, when he sitteth among the elders of the land."

It was only with the rise of the industrial revolution—and then only when it was in full swing and immigrants supplied adequate and cheap labor—that wives were viewed as full-time mothers and creators of a haven from a society that creates stress and strains. The current American family has a long way to go before it fully adjusts to these new and shifting work patterns. The greatest changes will be the reallocation of work responsibilities within households. A decrease of chores allocated along traditional sexist lines coupled with women sharing more effectively in the family decisionmaking process are the primary adjustments that will be made. Barring radical upheavals, both economic realities and social norms are likely to move, albeit ever so slowly, in this direction.

These changes in family work roles—unlike fads that come and go—will probably have some of the deepest and most lasting effects on the institution and upon American society. Instead of dissolution, they offer real opportunities for improved, more stable, and richer lives within families.

Chapter Six

FEMALE-HEADED FAMILIES

> Mrs. Boyle: We'll go. Come, Mary, an' we'll never
> come back. I've got a little room in me
> sister's where we'll stop till your trouble is
> over, an' then we'll work together for the
> sake of the baby.
>
> Mary: My poor little child that'll have no father!
>
> Mrs. Boyle: It'll have what's far better—it'll have two
> mothers.
>
> Sean O'Casey, *Juno and the Paycock*

MATRIARCHY

At one time the opinion expressed by Mrs. Boyle would not have been fit for respectable society. It still is far from being the majority point of view. Yet a growing number of American children are being raised in households that do not include their father or any other adult male. Exploited by TV shows and other media coverage, the female-headed household has become commonplace on the American scene.

Female-headed families are not a recent invention of the feminist movement. With high death rates in the past, it was not uncommon for a wife and mother to find herself a widow at a relatively young age, forced by this grim reality to take on the responsibilities of heading a household.

In fact, this event was so familiar that society invented a different set of mores for widows than for women who still lived with their husbands. For example, during the American colonial period a wife who ran a business concern was seldom socially acceptable. However, if her husband died, the community accepted her stepping in to run the family business.[1]

No Man at Home

Some social scientists have viewed female-headed families as a prime cause of sustained poverty for certain groups. The Moynihan Report is possibly the most publicized study supporting this hypothesis. Named after its chief author, Daniel P. Moynihan, and issued by the United States Labor Department in 1965 during the Johnson administration, this report concluded that "at the heart of the deterioration of the fabric of Negro society is the deterioration of the Negro family." The matriarchal structure that is "out of line with the rest of the American society seriously retards the progress of the group as a whole." According to Moynihan's interpretation, the data showed a strong correlation between academic failure, juvenile delinquency, crime, being rejected for military service, and being raised in a female-headed family. The report concluded that "Negro children without fathers flounder—and fail."[2] Black children whose fathers were not living at home were shown to be even more seriously disadvantaged than black children being raised in husband-wife families.

Besides a greater chance of destitution, female-headed families were cited by the Moynihan Report as being less able to pass on certain basic skills and values that are required if one is to function adequately within American society. Until the black family structure was stabilized and strengthened, many federal social welfare programs would run into serious roadblocks, the report asserted. The report favored programs that would foster stable husband-wife family patterns.

Needless to say the Moynihan Report was hardly universally accepted. Some criticized the report as a new and subtle form of racism. Instead of blaming outside cultural and economic factors for conditions within the black ghettos, critics charged that the report indicated that blacks themselves were responsible for their own poverty. Other critics insisted that the report drew dangerously inexact conclusions from weak and insufficient data, and that it made the naive error of linking causality with statistical relationships. Even if a causal relationship existed between poor social conditions and being raised in female-headed families, these findings might be the result of a cycle of poverty and not the cause of destitution.[3]

Other analysts charged that pathology is in the eye of the beholder.

They argued that what the Moynihan Report viewed with alarm was, in reality, a rational and alternative family system that was developed to meet the unique cultural needs of black society.

Arguing that black families display numerous "strengths," sociologist Robert B. Hill of the National Urban League has concluded that it is wrong to use a white family system as the measuring rod for black households. Hill's case rests on the following characteristics of the black family.

1. Strong kinship bonds—Black families show a high propensity to absorb other relatives into their households; for example, only about 7 percent of the black babies born out of wedlock each year are put up for formal adoption (versus about two-thirds of the white babies born in similar circumstances).

2. Strong work orientations—Despite low wages, poor working conditions, and few chances for advancement, roughly 60 percent of the females heading black families work during the year.

3. Adaptability of family roles—Contrary to claims of matriarchy, black families tend to be far more "equalitarian" than other ethnic group households.

4. Strong religious and achievement orientations—The church historically has been, and remains, a key institution within the black community, and it has had a major positive impact on black family life. Also, about three-fourths of the young blacks who enroll in college come from homes in which the family heads never went to institutions of longer learning.[4]

However, as Christopher Lasch has noted, holders of this opinion concerning black female-headed families would be in a far stronger position if they were backed up by the black community. As repeated investigations have shown, the vast majority of adult blacks (even female family heads) when questioned about the family system in which they would prefer to raise children still name the more traditional husband-wife households.[5] Of course, the bulk of husband-wife families have an income above the poverty threshold, which numerous two-parent black households have never crossed.

Whatever its merits, the Moynihan Report had a major impact on social policies during the Johnson administration. After the report was issued, President Johnson declared that a prime goal of the war on poverty would be "to strengthen the family and create conditions under which most parents will stay together." At the same time, the Moynihan thesis concerning the deterioration of the black husband-wife family strongly influenced the direction of the Great Society's antipoverty programs.[6]

Not Just the Ghetto

As the 1960s came to an end, the plight of black female-headed families was viewed as a serious problem. The debate continued: Some researchers viewed female-headed families as being a result of the culture of poverty, whereas others insisted that sustained discrimination was the cause of intergenerational destitution, which affected family stability, and was, therefore, foreign to the middle class and the white suburbs. Because of major shifting trends in divorce and family formation patterns, the experts—who were mostly white and middle class themselves—were in for a rude awakening. A researcher did not have to travel into a black urban ghetto to study female-headed families; they could be found along almost any tree-lined, split-level, affluent, suburban street.

An ironic twist was taking place in social theories that viewed the establishment of norms as a "trickling down" process, whereby the lower classes emulate and adopt the norms of the ruling class. Thorstein Veblen's theories on conspicuous consumption and Sinclair Lewis's ruminations about American midwestern main streets acutely had depicted this process. Family analysts, too, have noted this trickle down process; for example, family sociologist Ira Reiss has shown how many minority parents came to take on an earlier middle-class faith in longer education as a guarantor of success for their children.[7]

However, as social critic Tom Wolfe has noted, this trickle down process has been stood on its head within American society in recent years. In popular music, dress, drugs, and other forms of amusement and language, the bottom rungs have been the cultural pacemakers and trendsetters, Wolfe has argued. Black activist Eldridge Cleaver also has noted how the cultural emulation process has been reversed, with many young white adults trying to behave more like blacks.[8]

Matriarchy has become a growing feature of middle-class white society. The sheer increase in numbers of female-headed families is significant in itself, but the accompanying attitudinal changes are no less important. More women, and also men, now share the views expressed by Sean O'Casey's Mrs. Boyle concerning the legitimacy of the female-headed family. Having a man in the house is no longer regarded, according to this view, as a prerequisite to raising children, even if he is necessary for initiating the process—at least until test-tube babies become more commonplace.

Faced with continued exploitation within the traditional husband-wife family structure, some feminist publicists saw a male-free household as the only way they could improve and enrich their lives. Hence, feminism in the 1970s often seemed to be antifamily.[9] Some militant liberationists viewed the female-headed household not as an institution to be decried, but as a positive affirmation of a new lifestyle. But this was apparently only the first wave of the feminist movement. The "new agenda," Betty Friedan has noted, will be to enable women to live in equality with men under the same roof. Most often this will take the form of a husband-wife family, but living under different arrangements than the sexually stereotyped household of the past. Whether the future will conform to Friedan's vision remains to be seen.

It does appear that the female-headed family will remain a significant feature on the American scene for many years. Female-headed families, despite feminist advances, are still far more likely to be poor and to experience sustained economic hardship. Trying to be family head, mother, and an active member of the labor force has been a difficult challenge for most women. Working females who head households are at even a more serious disadvantage than other women.

Single-parent families tend, however, to be a temporary phenomenon. Data on the gross flows of women who become family heads indicate that this condition is for many females only a way station. Still, the conditions experienced by women who head families, and their children, present serious problems covering a range of social issues from welfare to labor market discrimination. A large portion of these women have found it impossible to pull their families out of poverty without government help.

A NEW WAVE?

Since the New Deal initiated the welfare state, the total number of American families has more than doubled, but the number headed by women has more than tripled, accelerating during the 1970s. At the start of the 1970s nearly one of ten families was headed by women; this ratio rose to one of seven families by the close of the decade, when over 8 million women headed families (figure 14). Altogether, these families accounted for 26 million persons including 12 million children (in 6 million of the families). Seventeen percent of all American children are being raised in a female-headed family, compared with 10 percent in 1970.

Black children are still far more likely to live in a female-headed home than are white youngsters. In 1980, half of all black children

FIGURE 14.

The percent of female family heads is rising.

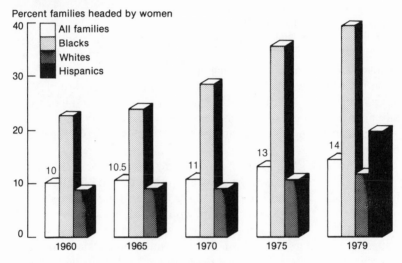

Source: U.S., Department of Commerce, Bureau of the Census

were being raised in a household headed by a woman compared with 12 percent of all white children. A Hispanic youngster had about a 20 percent chance of living in this type of household.

The reasons families had a female head also changed during the 1970s. As noted, historically widows have represented the largest proportion of women who head families. At the start of the 1970s roughly 43 percent of female family heads were widows, twice the proportion who were divorced. By the end of the decade, divorced women accounted for 34 percent of all women who headed families, while widows represented 29 percent of the total. The relative rate of women who had never married and were heading a family had doubled during this period.

However, the rising incidence of families headed by women is not due exclusively to increasing marital instability or illegitimacy.

An estimated two-fifths of the nearly 2 million additional female-headed families formed between 1940 and 1970 have been attributed to an increased propensity to form separate households rather than sharing housing with relatives. This pattern continued during the 1970s. Income-support programs may also have boosted the growing ranks of female-headed families, as did declining childlessness and, of course, general population increases.

Economic Realities

Of the major differences existing between female-headed and husband-wife households, those based on income are easiest to quantify. Poverty haunts only 1 of 19 husband-wife families; 1 of 9 families maintained by men who never married or are separated, divorced, or widowed; but about 1 of 3 female-headed families.

Beyond the higher prevalence of poverty, the entire income distribution of families headed by women is lower than that of other kinds of families. In 1978, less than 19 percent of the families headed by women had earned incomes as high as $15,000, compared with more than 60 percent of all husband-wife families and 48 percent

Burdens
of the Black Female
Family Head

FIGURE 15.

The income distribution of female-headed families is highly skewed toward the low end of the spectrum (1978).

Female-headed families

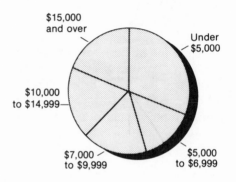

Husband-wife families

Male-headed families

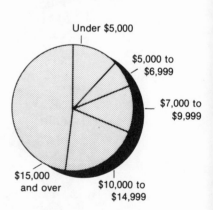

Source: U.S., Department of Commerce, Bureau of the Census

of families headed by men. While the income distribution of husband-wife families, and even households headed by men, are skewed toward the upper end, the distribution pattern is reversed for female-headed families (figure 15).

The median income of female-headed families is less than half that of husband-wife households. Where dependent children are involved, the median drops to one-third. If a female family head has a child under 6 years, her family income on average is only two-fifths of that for a female-headed household with no youngsters.

Coupled with this factor are the younger ages of the women who are heading families. At the start of the 1970s, women under 25 represented about 7 percent of all female family heads, but by the close of the decade about 10 percent were under 25. About 1 of 4 women who headed families were between the ages 25 and 34—the second most likely group to have very young children. The proportion of women in the older age groups has, of course, diminished.

National longitudinal data, which have followed female cohorts for several years, have increased our knowledge about these families. Data tracking the same women—as they go through a dissolution of a husband-wife family and then try making it on their own—give a clearer picture of this dynamic process than information based on cross-sectional estimates. The National Longitudinal Surveys (NLS) at Ohio State University included interviews with a nationally representative sample of over 5,000 women, consisting of women under 25 years of age and 30 to 44 years of age at the time of the first interview (1967 and 1968, respectively). These women were interviewed annually or biennially, sometimes in person and sometimes by telephone, and the data provide a time path of their experiences over ten years. Some of the most important features indicated by the NLS concerning female-headed families include the following.[10]

1. Few women remain heads of households for an extended period of time. Over the first five years, the surveys found that as many as 16 percent of all adult women sampled were heading a household. However, only 9 percent were household heads during the entire period; 6 percent of the white women and 21 percent of black women. Hence, there is a large flow of women who move into and out of being a female-family head.

2. The transition from a husband-wife family to a female-headed unit often creates dire economic problems, which the women who head the new households often cannot solve without outside aid. For the older age cohort, the average household income for white families that experienced this disruption declined by 49 percent,

and, while average black household income fell by only 38 percent, their income prior to disruption of the family was only about two-thirds of the average for the white households. This same condition is also true for women in the younger age cohort. For younger white women who experienced a disruption, household income fell by 60 percent; for younger black women the decline was 58 percent. The economic jolt for younger women—who have a greater chance of being mothers of young children—was even greater than for older females.

Cross-sectional data from the Current Population Survey back up these findings concerning economic hardship. If a white woman is not a family head, her chances of living in poverty (which was $7,400 or under for a family of four in 1980) are less than 1 of 20. If she becomes a family head, her chances of living in destitution rise to nearly one of four. Even if a black woman is not a family head, her chances of living in poverty are about one of four, but if she heads a family, they exceed one of two.

3. Labor force patterns of women who experience marital disruption are quite different for whites and blacks for both the younger and older women. When their marriage ended, the older cohort of white wives in the NLS survey increased their labor force participation rate from 58 percent to 70 percent. For black women just the opposite happened. Their rate fell from more than 80 percent to 69 percent. Transition patterns also differ for black and white women concerning their seeking occupational training. When they became family heads, the number of the older women who obtained training increased by more than 40 percent for whites but fell by 37 percent for blacks. For younger white women the labor force participation rate climbed from 51 percent to 68 percent after the disruption. For younger black women, unlike their older counterparts, the rate did not decline upon divorce, but it rose much less than for the young white women—from 46 percent to 53 percent. For younger white women after a divorce, the chances of resorting to training increased by 23 percent, while for younger black women it fell by 13 percent.

Several factors help explain why the transition from living with a husband to becoming head of one's own household vastly increases employment for white women, decreases the chances for mature black females, and has only a minor impact on younger black women. A far greater proportion of black family heads have not finished high school. Almost two-thirds of the black female family heads in the NLS sample had not completed high school compared with one-third of the white women. This educational difference made it more difficult for black women to land better paying jobs. Since the rewards from work would be lower, it is understandable why the reaction of black women is different compared to white. The black woman who heads a household was doubly disadvantaged because she also had a greater chance than the white woman of having a serious health problem: about one of three, compared with only about one of five, respectively. Health problems are more prevalent among women who are heading families than among the rest of the adult female population.

Though the statistics suggest that health and education explain much of the labor force differences between white and black female family heads, racial discrimination must also be considered. NLS data indicate that black female heads are much more likely to be relegated to physically demanding jobs. Almost two-thirds of the white female heads who are employed, but only one-fourth of the blacks, have white-collar jobs. Thus, bad health is potentially a greater roadblock to employment for blacks since they usually get jobs with greater physical demands. Also, even if a black woman finds employment, she can expect a wage rate about 10 percent lower than that for a white woman. The black female head also has a far greater chance that children will be living in her house. With their lower earnings and their greater child-related responsibilities, fewer black female heads have been able to enter the labor market and earn a living.

Even if a female family head lands a job, her earnings are not likely to make up for the income lost because a husband has left. According to NLS data, average per capita income will decline by 20 percent for white families and 13 percent for black families.[11]

4. Female-headed families depend more upon transfer payments than other types of families as a major source of household income. About 16 percent of all white female heads and 48 percent of black female heads recieve AFDC or other public welfare payments. Over 23 percent of the white female heads, and 19 percent of the black women heads, received social security or disability payments. One-third of poor white female heads, and more than 50 percent of poor black female heads, received at least half of their household income from public income transfer programs. On the average, earnings by a female head provided only about one-third of household income for families living in poverty and about three-fifths for those above the poverty line. One-quarter of all black female-headed households had no wage earners, compared with about one-sixth of their white counterparts. For about 10 percent of all female-headed families

public transfer payments represented their major source of income: Over a five-year period, the NLS survey found that about 50 percent of the white female family heads who did not remarry were in poverty for at least one year; about 15 percent were continuously poor. For black heads who did not remarry the situation was even worse; the comparable figures were over 40 percent and about 25 percent, respectively.[12]

Thus, whatever other advantages a woman perceives in single parenthood over a bad marriage, most female-headed families find the going is very rough economically. Even when they combine work with welfare and other transfer payments, many female heads can barely lift their families out of poverty—and a significant number must live below the poverty threshold. Either by choice or by circumstances beyond their control, a growing number of households are being run without the full-time presence of a man. The most important question is whether the 1970s—the years of rapid growth in female-headed families—represents an aberration or a harbinger of things to come.

A TRANSITIONAL PHASE?

Not only has the incidence of female-headed families grown in recent years but the reasons for their prevalence have changed radically. First, widowhood is no longer the prime factor causing women to head their own households. As a result the average age of these female family heads has declined, and the chances are far greater that her household also includes children under 6 years of age. This phenomenon has become pervasive throughout all sectors of society. Second, a growing number of these households appear to have formed out of free choice as an increasing number of women have opted for operating their own households.

The word *family* used to evoke a picture of a husband, a wife, and their children living together in one household. Now, a variety of cameos surround the central picture. None of the cameos, however, portrays the extended family that many analysts had anticipated because they believed a separated women would return to her parents' or grandparents' household, taking her children with her. An increasing percentage of never-married or formerly married mothers are heading their own households instead of living as a subfamily unit in someone else's household, emphasizing the precarious status of female-headed families. In extended families a divorced, separated, or never-married mother could count on the financial and social support of other adult family members to help provide for basic needs and ease such problems as child care. Historians still argue about how strong a hold the extended family ever had in the United States.[13] Whatever happened in the past, the chances are that if a woman currently decides to go her own way, she will have to head her own household.

Liberation within Families?

There are some early indications that the increase in the single-parent household will not be as swift in the 1980s as in the 1960s and 1970s. A process of stabilization may be taking place that will mitigate the upsurge of female-headed families in the near future. The view asserted by some early feminists that the woman should seek liberation outside a husband-wife family is not shared by the vast majority of female family heads. As Elaine Morgan put it: "The more way-out liberationists seem hell-bent on destroying the institution . . . .When we're just getting loose of one lot of people laying down the law that we must get married, it's a bit rough to run head on into another lot telling us we mustn't. Anyway, marriage is going to be with us for a long time yet."[14]

Heather Ross and Isabel Sawhill have used a model of female-headed households with many interesting parallels to American labor markets. Similar to the labor force behavior, turnover rates and mobility appear to be high.[15] Nor is it correct to conclude that those women who remain family heads do so by choice. When questioned, long-term female family heads most often indicated that their current household structure is not their first choice.[16] Although some feminists understandably viewed being the heads of their own household as an acceptable road to liberation, women who follow that road seldom achieve liberation. Simone de Beauvoir noted that only the highly trained professional woman and the highly placed woman in business could attain a position of independence and equality in a male-dominated world.[17]

The alternative to the traditional patriarchal family does not have to be a female-headed household with no adult males, according to a growing number of feminist critics. They are not lessening their attack on certain features of the traditional household, but merely advocating different means of achieving these ends.[18]

Even if female-headed families remain a transitional phase for most, and even if the growth of this household type diminishes, a significant number of youngsters will continue to spend some of their childhood in this family structure. Because of the deep-rooted problems experienced by women who head families, public policy must be concerned with easing and improving this transition. However, the most important family-related changes in the future are likely to occur within the more traditional family structure and public policy will focus on smoothing these changes.

Part Three

FAMILY POLICIES: SHORING UP THE HAVEN?

Chapter Seven

THE FAMILY IN THE WELFARE STATE

> *Blanche Dubois:* I have always depended on the
> kindness of strangers.
> Tennessee Williams, *A Streetcar Named Desire*

PROBLEMS AND POLICIES

In the past the family may not always have been the best haven from a heartless world, as Blanche Dubois discovered, but it was the main mechanism of support in times of trouble. However, economic and social changes in many cases have shifted responsibilities for individuals in need from the family to the state. Numerous families in the welfare state now depend on the impersonal kindness of strangers to help them cope and retain viable households.

Adjustments to dramatic economic and social changes never have been easy. During the initial wave of industrialization workers may have obtained a higher standard of living, but at the cost of altered living and household arrangements. Older supporting mechanisms could not function in this new environment.

Josiah Wedgwood, one of England's pioneering industrial entrepreneurs, reportedly told disgruntled employees to ask their parents for a realistic description of living conditions prior to the industrial revolution and then compare those accounts with their present state. The comparisons could only be highly favorable toward life under the then new and emerging mode of production, Wedgwood fer-

121

vently believed.[1] It is not as clear whether Wedgwood's workers saw the situation in the same light.

While industrialization created the conditions for rapid economic growth and rising living standards, it also brought new problems. The establishment of national markets and large urban factories made employment and wages highly dependent upon the vagaries of new economic forces; the unpredictable and invisible hand could decimate as well as uplift. Also, the factory system tended to depersonalize the relationship between employer and workers. Industrialization often reduced the skill level and social status of labor. A growing number of workers were required to uproot themselves and leave the land for jobs in the expanding factories located in urban centers.

Nuclear Families

The economic and social transformations fostered a rapid rise in the gross national product, but at a considerable toll. A growing urban poor population and the destruction of established household patterns were byproducts of these changes. There is a growing debate among historians as to how extensive the extended family was in American society, and it appears to have been much more common in Europe than in the New World, because many of the immigrants in America were younger adults who left their parents and most other kin in their native countries.

"Our family is very secure, except for the possibility of death, illness, unemployment, separation or divorce."

However, when the United States was an agricultural society dotted with villages and small towns, it was not uncommon to find three generations all living under the same roof. But since relatively few people lived beyond the biblical threescore and ten, and most died at a much younger age—as late as 1920 life expectancy at birth was 54 years—demographic factors suggest that sustained three-generation families could not have been widespread. In this environment, trades and skills were passed down from parent to child, and the extended family also shouldered the responsibility for the care of its elderly members and other relatives who could not fend for themselves. The rural family was often almost self-sufficient. Even when trading with the rest of the community, a family enterprise involved almost all its members.[2] The family filled the primary roles as provider of economic necessities and education. In addition to its varied functions, the family in effect was a social security system.

As the industrial revolution progressed, the family was overshadowed by other institutions in performing some of its earlier functions. Economic production moved from household to factory. New and expanding manufacturing industries required a mobile labor force, and people moved where the jobs were. Beyond employment, the social surplus generated by the highly productive industrial sector provided the resources to create public education, health care and other institutions. Providing basic education to all youngsters was one of the first major family activities in which the government became involved. Before the New Deal in America—or Bismarck in Germany and Lloyd George in England—the options were work, starve, or turn to one's family for support. Now with a vast web of income transfer and in-kind programs, an individual has many more options.

Many roles undertaken by the modern welfare state were at one time the major responsibility of the family. In fact, the founding fathers in framing the Constitution did not assign to the federal government any jurisdiction over family affairs. The various states were given the powers to pass "family laws" covering sex, marriage, responsibility for rearing children, and divorce, and it was assumed that government regulation of these essentially personal affairs would be kept to a minimum.

While the extended family, even when it existed, was often not the wellspring of bucolic bliss depicted by some fertile romantic minds, it had several qualities that the more urban nuclear family could not match. Compared with the extended family, the nuclear family had a much higher potential of being unstable. With more adults in the household, the extended family could absorb added responsibilities created by the death, illness, unemployment, separation, or divorce of one member, whereas a similar tragedy could crush the smaller nuclear unit. Thus, the nuclear family in the industrialized world had lost many of the traditional supports of the past.[3] These families were playing a game of chance. If the breadwinner could hang on to a stable job with good pay, the household would be a winner compared with extended families or rural life. However, if the breadwinner died or had some mishap, then the members of the nuclear family could experience a more wrenching form of destitution than they would have endured within extended family units.

High mobility may have increased the possibilities for better jobs, but it has often reduced family and community ties and increased the sense of alienation and loneliness. As an indication of the rapid residential mobility within the population, the average American moves 14 times in his or her lifetime, and roughly one of five Americans moves each year.

As mobility reduced the roles played by the family, the void was seldom filled by other private institutions, so the government established programs to shoulder some of the responsibilities once performed by the family. Most of these programs were designed to cure a specific social pathology—such as destitution among the elderly population—and no real thought was given as to how a specific program would link up or interrelate with other policies affecting families.[4] For better or for worse the welfare state has become an integral part of our economy and society. This institutional change has had a dramatic impact on American family life.

Toward a Comprehensive Policy?

Although the champions of a comprehensive family policy—whatever that may mean—continue to be heard, the government has tended to step into family situations only when families have failed or are being failed. Campaigning for the presidency in 1976, Jimmy Carter expressed a deep concern about the "loss of stability and the loss of values" within American society. The root cause of this problem was "the steady erosion and weakening of our families," he asserted.[5] The solution, Carter insisted, was to design a strong "pro-family" policy that would encourage families to remain together. Such a policy would include a system of income transfers that would raise families out of destitution, encourage work, and provide the in-kind goods and services required to stabilize family life. Our lack of a formal comprehensive family policy was the "same thing as an antifamily policy," he asserted. In the name of a strong "pro-family" policy, Ronald Reagan campaigned during the 1980 election on a platform that opposed the Equal Rights Amendment and abortion and favored prayer in public schools. His position in each case would lead to stronger and more stable families, Reagan insisted.

Presidents Carter and Reagan touched on what appears to be a very sensitive theme; issues concerning the future of the American family have become controversial political items. But needless to say, neither spelled out what would constitute the complete elements of a comprehensive pro-family policy. While some advocates call for the creation of new programs to improve family life, some critics argue that the welfare state has contributed to the erosion of the work ethic and caused some of the difficulties experienced by American families. Welfare, the opponents charge, has led not only to family breakups, encouraging husbands to desert their wives and fathers to leave their children, but it has also made bearing children out of wedlock profitable. The criticisms take a variety of twists and turns, each faulting the welfare state and its presumed deleterious impact on the family. One analyst has asserted that the welfare state has created a new class of "helping professionals" who have taken over too many parenthood and family life responsibilities.[6] The assumption has been that social engineering directed by this new class has been expanded into more and more activities once left to individuals and their families, on the assumption that these helping professionals can do a better job than the one "wretchedly performed by most parents." But, instead of improving conditions, these social engineers have left families less able to cope in the world and even more dependent on the services provided by this new class. Just as the rural family became dependent upon a highly complex food distribution system, today's family must seek a growing list of supporting services outside the home. Despite good intentions, according to this formulation, the welfare state has weakened the family and forced it to turn to public resources.

America does not appear to be alone in this trend, nor has it even been the leader. In France, helping professionals started to exert an enormous influence on family life before a similar trend was established in the United States.[7]

In a presumably conservative era, a growing number of critics have questioned the efficacy and desirability of many government efforts. However, it appears that governmental activities affecting households were more a response to, than a cause of, changing living conditions. The breakdown of the extended family preceded the establishment of the social security system in the 1930s. Payments to the elderly may have given more senior citizens the chance to maintain households independent of their children, but this freedom of choice can have many social benefits for individuals and society. It is far easier to damn the growth of the welfare state than to fashion realistic social, political, and economic alternatives. Faced with having their mother-in-law move in with them, many critics apparently would prefer the separate living arrangements made possible by the social security system. Given the current distribution of the total economic pie, one may wonder whether American family life would be measurably improved if the assistance provided by the welfare state were eliminated or vastly reduced. In most cases, government action was required because numerous families did not have the resources to cope with dire problems affecting their households. Far from leading to a weakening of family bonds, the welfare state enabled many families to remain together.

It would be more persuasive to argue that all too often the programs designed by the welfare state ignore the fact that most people live in families. For example, analysis of labor force measurements count individuals as employed, unemployed, or not in the labor force, too frequently ignoring the economic status of their families. The official statistics count the unemployed worker who is the sole support of a household the same as the one who lives in a household with a total income that exceeds the national median. Economic hardship can only be understood when one considers not only the work experience of the individual but the total family income. Many government social programs set their goals, collect data, and provide benefits on the basis of individual needs and do not consider the larger picture of household living conditions.

Surveys of American attitudes show highly conflicting views about the relationship of the welfare state and family policy. One national sample found that four of five individuals thought that the federal government is spending too much money. However, when questioned about specific social and family related areas as health, education, and housing, the vast majority said that the federal government should allocate more funds in each case.[8] Given this American love-hate relationship with government, it is understandable why calls to reduce government involvement in people's lives have directly coincided with a mounting effort to expand social programs.

It is easy to call for a coordinated pro-family policy on the campaign trail or during congressional oversight hearings. However, it is much more difficult to propose an acceptable package of programs that would win a consensus. As Martin Rein has noted, "government cannot affirm its objectives, because it cannot articulate the normative direction toward which it is moving."[9] Given our highly pluralistic society, there is little likelihood that a consensus will develop on a single comprehensive policy for the family.

Policymakers may agree on the desirablility of "stabilizing" the family, but they may differ sharply on the type of family that the government should stabilize. Some would tilt government policies in favor of households in which a husband is the sole breadwinner supporting a full-time housewife and several children. When the ethos was to move into suburbia and live the "good life," it appeared sound social policy to pass legislation favoring home ownership and a highway system that made suburban family life possible. Tax laws, social security, and other government benefits and obligations were structured in such a way that they encouraged household formations agreeing with this once-predominant social norm.

However, social norms have become highly diverse, and prospective changes in the structure of American families may increase this diversity. Husband-wife couples, who made up about 75 percent of all households in 1960, comprised less than 65 percent of the total by the end of the 1970s and may represent only 55 percent of all American households by 1990. Even within husband-wife families there have been major changes, and more can be expected. By 1990 only about half of all married couples may have children under 15 years of age in the house, comprising one of every four households, instead of the three of seven ratio that prevailed in 1960, and one of three in 1978.[10]

With these changes in mind, should policies encourage a return to the family as it existed in the 1950s, or should they support and encourage currently diverse preferences? The appropriate answers are not at all clear. Some traditionalists view adjustment of our institutions—including education, social security, tax laws, health care system—to accommodate the new forces as fueling the fire that is destroying once widely held norms that they believe should be supported and sustained. Others believe that it is neither wise nor even possible to reverse the current trends in living arrangements, arguing that family policy should be neutral and even-handed to all types of household arrangements, thus avoiding the need to specify what type of family life the government is trying to stabilize. Still others want a family policy that is neither neutral nor protective of traditions; they advocate policies that would speed up the changes; or even would make it easier to split up a husband-wife family.[11]

If strict neutrality sounds like a worthwhile goal in relation to household types, then the specifics must be considered. Should families that have children be expected to pay the same taxes as childless households that have the same income? Or should home-owning families receive favorable tax treatment vis-à-vis renting families? Strict neutrality may appeal in principle, but it would gore some favorite oxen.

The 1980 White House Conference on Families has demonstrated the difficulties of reaching a consensus on specific areas of a family policy.[12] Considering that family issues and values are deeply personal matters, and given the wide diversity of social norms, it is difficult to hammer out even general goals and objectives.

Even if the ends could be agreed upon, questions would arise concerning the means of attaining these objectives. For example, how would fertility or divorce rates respond to specified shifts in the tax code? For that matter, can any legislative enactments change the basic trends that have affected American family life? Government actions *do*, of course, have a profound impact on many aspects of daily living within households, but there are limits as to what can be realistically accomplished within constitutional constraints. And the experience with the proposed Equal Rights Amendment shows the obstacles to achieving some consensus by way of constitutional change.

What about Other Countries?

An examination of several foreign countries' experiences with family policies demonstrates real differences in the pathologies that were highlighted for remedial treatment, compared with current conditions in the United States. The Scandinavian countries are often cited as models of a family policy. However, close examination of the direction taken in these countries indicates that it would be difficult and probably undesirable to duplicate similar programs in the United States.

While they may be currently called family policies in the Scandinavian nations, these programs were almost always labeled as population policies by their original advocates. In Sweden, Gunnar and Alva Myrdal were among the first and most persuasive advocates of policies to increase the annual crop of babies. During the 1930s, Swedish economists and sociologists experienced dramatic changes in their views regarding demographic growth. Prior to the Great Depression, social scientists in Sweden shared the belief that their country would be facing problems associated with overpopulation. Toward the end of the 1800s, the renowned Swedish economist Knut Wicksell launched a major campaign that made Malthusian population theory a topic of household conversation. Wicksell was concerned that if their population continued to grow unchecked, Scandinavian countries would not be able to feed their citizenry and that their per capita income would plummet as population increases would vastly outstrip the realistic prospects for economic growth.

Initially Wicksell's views received a cold reception, and he was threatened with the loss of his academic post for pressing his unpopular population theories. However, in time his views were accepted, and they became the dominant viewpoint.[13] It could be argued that his Malthusian preachments were so persuasive as to halt population growth. But, without denying the might of the pen, it seems that world economic depression and other factors associated with industrialization may have had a greater impact on population trends than the scholarly debates. The Swedish fertility rate declined and—coupled with migration—threatened a population decline.

Whatever the causes of the declining birth rate, by the 1930s the problem was the opposite from what Wicksell had posed. Nor were the changed conditions only the concern of technical experts and policymakers. Alva Myrdal observed that the situation raised deep emotional and ideological conflicts. Many feared that the decline was destined to take the form of an "incessant and self-perpetuating liquidation of the people."[14] The population issue was viewed as a concern affecting all of society. The outcome could not be left to chance or some invisible hand, and active government policies were viewed as a necessity even by conservative political circles within these countries. Fears about depopulation "acted as a godfather" to Scandanavian family policies.[15]

Beyond national pride, the threat of depopulation posed other serious problems to the Scandinavian nations. The revolution in demographic thought coincided with the rising influence of Keynesian macroeconomic ideas. Declines in population could be a major force halting economic development and causing long-term economic stagnation. A population reversal would reduce demand for goods and services, and it would harshly dampen capital investment in new technology. It would also have the effect in the long run of producing dire labor shortages, and it could make a country more highly dependent upon other nations.[16] Moved by these concerns, most of the Scandinavian nations established high ranking government commissions to explore policies that might lead to population growth.

The policies, whose initial impetus was a concern over population growth, resulted in expansion of the welfare state. The rationale behind reducing the financial costs of having and rearing children was that if the price of progeny were lowered, potential parents would have more children, just as they would presumably buy more of any other commodity is its price were marked down. A 1937 law provided free maternity, obstetrical services, and child-health care. Government backed low-cost loans for home furnishings and other items were also made to newly married couples. In 1948 these efforts were expanded to include universal family allowances to support all children up to the age of 16, apparently with little consideration that the meager allowances could hardly encourage greater fertility among the affluent. Later, the system was amended to include a rent allowance for households with children, and a supplemental formula was devised to provide a larger allowance to destitute families.[17]

All of the developed industrial countries, except the United States, have family allowance systems providing some modest payments regardless of family income. Because the allowances are most often universal, the actual cash value has often remained small—typically between 5 to 10 percent of a country's median wage for one child and slightly higher for more youngsters.[18]

Population policy advocates, such as the Myrdals, were interested not only in quantity but also in the quality of the next generation. Family planning support was provided to avert the birth of more unwanted children. Once the children were born the next step was to improve the environment in which children were raised. The goal of the emerging welfare state was to assure that all goods and services deemed essential for parents and children would become either free or subsidized.

Family policy in Sweden in the 1970s branched out to consider other problems such as sexual equality in households. As in the United States, the Swedish tax code was based on the assumption of a household consisting of one male worker, a full-time housewife, and one or more children, but this model became less representative as women entered the labor force. To end what was, in effect, a marriage tax penalty, the Swedish tax code was revised in the 1970s to allow individual taxation for husband-wife families.

To assist or encourage women to enter the labor force, Sweden also expanded its child care services, but the demand still exceeds the supply. In 1974, a "child leave" system was also instituted that entitled gainfully employed parents to divide 9 months of child care leave during which they receive 90 percent of their regular income. Thus, during the 1970s Swedish social welfare efforts were revised to better reflect the gradual replacement of the one-earner family by the two-breadwinner household.

Should the United States emulate this model of a family policy? To be sure, many of its features could be included in American social welfare programs. For example, as far as the U.S. Internal Revenue Service is concerned, two cannot always live as cheaply as one; multi–pay check families often pay higher income taxes than they would if they were not married and had the same total income. However, the United States is far more heterogeneous than other industrialized nations. It is also appears to lack any specific central unifying principle, such as the former depopulation fears of other nations, which could unite American concerns in this area. Considering U.S. concerns about the limits to growth and environmental factors, it does not appear that pronatalist policies could provide the key spark to motivate an integrated American family policy. The emotional hassles generated by the 1980 White House family conferences are ample evidence of the concerns and obstacles that lie in the path of any attempt to formulate a consensus on a family policy.

West Germany does provide an example of how other concerns can result in the formation of family policies. After World War II, it appeared to policymakers that the only German institution that remained firm despite the devastation was the family. As it appeared to be in relatively good shape, it was decided that the family should be used as a healthy building block in the foundation of efforts to revitalize the country. While Americans express many anxieties regarding modern family life, no one family issue or group of issues has captivated our attention the way fertility rates (or postwar fears in Germany) provided a springboard for other nations.

Instead of designing an explicitly coordinated family policy, the American welfare state has settled for a series of disparate programs that affect families. Avoiding a grand design, these programs are expanding gradually and incrementally, and they are adapting to the changing needs. Underlying the diverse proposals, but modest programmatic efforts, is the recognition that, for better or worse, American families will remain in a period of transition, and the resulting society will continue to have highly pluralistic living arrangements. This view, however, is not universally accepted, and voices are raised championing family policies suitable for a puritanical or Victorian society.

What can be accomplished is an easing of the period of transition by active social policies that seek to provide a basic living standard and essential services for all types of families. Such a policy would ensure that children are not raised in deprivation; it would keep them dry, warm, and fed no matter what type of household they live in. A realistic approach to these problems would be first to examine the already existing social efforts in these areas, and then to determine what changes are desirable and probable.

PROGRAMS AFFECTING FAMILIES

The United States may lack a coordinated family policy, but the government has instituted myriad programs that affect households. The Family Impact Seminar of the George Washington University has found 270 different federal programs, administered by 17 different departments and agencies, that have a direct impact on American families.[19] Any family that pays taxes, receives benefits or contributes to the government's massive income transfer system, or is involved with the public schools or courts, or seeks employment, training, or other social services is touched in some way by the far-reaching welfare state. Indeed, it seems almost impossible to establish policies that do not affect families. Like Molière's hero who spoke prose all his life but was not aware of the fact, American policymakers keep on designing new programs without recognizing their family implications.

The programs' basic assumptions about family life, however, often have been hidden and not fully stated. Assumptions that may have made sense during the 1930s may no longer reflect the shifting conditions and social mores that prevail today. Sometimes policymakers have ignored the ramifications of specific programs. Few politicians are on record as favoring policies that discourage marriage, but, as noted earlier, some programs may have such an impact.

Programs aimed at solving a specific problem unrelated to families may nevertheless have a tangential impact upon them. Reducing youth unemployment and retraining workers displaced by technological changes have been the goals of several government efforts.

That the alleviation of these problems also could have a beneficial impact on American family life cannot be denied because workers with stable and sufficient earnings may be in a better position to lead stable family lives. However, family-related objectives often have not been explicitly considered in these programs, as their design or evaluation have tended to view the target population only as individuals and not as members of household units.

Basic Needs

In the welfare state, the concept of what constitutes basic needs is continually expanding to include food, income, health care, shelter, education, social services, and even assistance for heating homes. The Social Security Act of 1935 has been the cornerstone in this effort. In fashioning this legislation, the Roosevelt administration and Congress concluded that shifting economic and social realities had created conditions requiring federal intervention, because the then-existing arrangements of mutual aid—including family, private, and local assistance—could not meet the complex needs of an advanced industrialized society.[20] The diminished nuclear family could not cope on its own with major bouts of massive unemployment or other disasters causing the loss of income. In the early stages of drafting the proposal, some New Dealers advocated a social security system that included provision for family subsidy, health care, and maternity benefits. However, the final package was much less ambitious and limited to what were then considered basic necessities.

It remained for later generations to expand the definition of basic needs. Helping all families to obtain minimal adequate living conditions requires a sustained long-term effort. The problems faced by many households in need are due not so much to cyclical slumps in economic conditions as to deep-rooted structural problems within society. Efforts to provide the basics for all households and to raise families out of poverty have met with some success. Poverty has been significantly reduced, even through liberals and conservatives may argue a good deal over the specifics.

Despite conceptual and technical problems of measurement, the federal government has devised a poverty index that has gained wide acceptance. The index reflects the different consumption requirements of families based on size and composition, sex and age of the family head, and farm and nonfarm residence. The 1981 poverty thresholds follow:

Number of family members	Nonfarm
1	$3,800
2	4,900
3	5,800
4	7,400
5	8,800
6	9,900

The number of families in destitution declined significantly during the 1960s and 1970s. While more than one of every five families were poor at the start of the 1960s, this level had fallen to one of ten two decades later. But these gains were not evenly distributed by size or type of family. The chances of being in poverty are highly related to family structure. More than one-third of female-headed families remain poor, as do more than one-seventh of families with children under 18 (figure 16).

The population of families in poverty also demonstrates other important differences in personal characteristics when compared with all American families. About one of four heads of poverty households completed fewer than eight years of elementary school education, compared with only about one of ten for all household heads. Place of residence also affects the incidence of destitution within families. Rural families face a much higher chance of living in destitution than do urban households. Husband-wife families experience a lower poverty rate than other family types. However, of the 5 million families classified in 1979 as living in poverty, 46 percent were husband-wife families, 51 percent were headed by females, and the remainder were male-headed families with no wife present.[21]

The principal economic support of almost 30 percent of all American families no longer comes from the earnings of a male head. This, of course, is due to several reasons. In about 14 percent of families, there is no male head to provide any support. Also, with an increased percentage of wives in the work force, their earnings plus earnings of other family members may exceed that of the traditional provider.[22]

Having an employed head may reduce the probability that a family will be in destitution, yet many heads are among the ranks of the working poor. A job for these working poor heads—even full-time employment—is no sure escape from poverty. About half of the heads of poverty households work during the year, and nearly 1 million of them work full time, full year.

FIGURE 16.

Despite improvement, about one of ten families still lives in poverty.

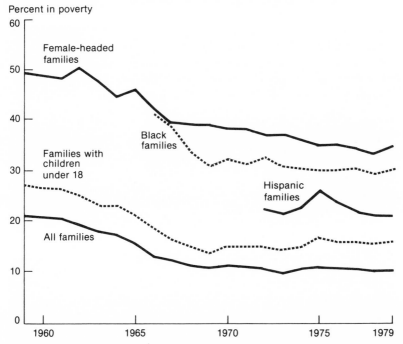

Source: U.S., Department of Commerce, Bureau of the Census

Alternative definitions and concepts have a major impact on poverty estimates. The Congressional Budget Office (CBO) has estimated that in the absence of government transfer payments about 25 percent of all American families would have been in poverty during 1976. However, government cash transfers are included in the official poverty index, and this inclusion reduced the proportion of destitute American families to about 10 percent. If in-kind programs were included, such as subsidized housing and food stamps, then the percentage in poverty would be reduced even further.[23]

Government programs may not have eliminated poverty within

all families, but they have vastly reduced the chances for almost all types of households. Destitution has been most highly reduced among households with heads 65 and over. Close to 1 million poor families are headed by an elderly adult. Without government transfer payments the number of poverty families with an elderly head would have been 60 percent greater, and the number of destitute families headed by females would have been almost 25 percent greater.[24] While the free market has continually reduced the proportion of families living below the official poverty threshold, many more households would have been counted among the poor in the absence of governmental intervention.

The welfare state has done, however, very little to aid two-parent families with children. Low-income families are frequently driven into poverty by the addition of family members (figure 17). Indeed,

FIGURE 17.

Larger families faced a greater risk of economic hardship (1979).

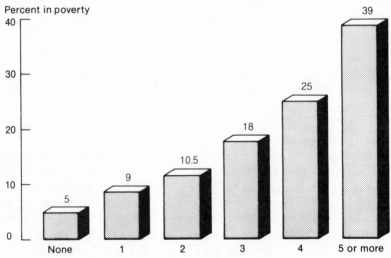

Source: U.S., Department of Commerce, Bureau of the Census

family size and poverty are closely related, with 57 percent of poor children coming from families with five or more members. A higher incidence of poverty among larger families is to be expected in a society where need is ignored as a factor in wage determination and where the necessity of child care often hinders the wife or female family head from earning needed income. As noted earlier, the United States is the only major industrial nation that makes no provision for family allowances.

In general, government policies to help the poor include four types of programs: (1) cash support; (2) direct provisions of necessities such as food, shelter, and medical care; (3) preventive and compensatory efforts for children and youth; and (4) attempts to restructure existing institutions to help families adapt to those institutions.

Various categories of families have different needs. Family heads and young people with their life's work ahead of them must have not only mere daily subsistence but also encouragement and support for acquiring the skills sought by employers. For the aged and their families, medical care and nursing homes are of primary concern. Children also need health care and the basic education to assure them opportunities in the future.

Also, certain services, such as child care, are being demanded by families with incomes higher than the median. Government social welfare efforts and the system used to finance these efforts have a pervasive impact on family decisions. Government policies may affect the choice of a place of residence or the decision to purchase or rent shelter, and may have an impact on the determination to marry. The financial prospects of ending a marriage can be altered by government transfer payments and in-kind aid programs. Whether one enters the labor market could well depend on the governmental child care policies in many cases. This is not to say that people act like cold computers and just calculate economic costs and benefits before they make decisions regarding love, marriage, and family life. Any analysis that ignores the irrational and emotional aspects bound up in these decisions is likely to be off the mark. However, households cannot totally ignore the impact of government policies.

Realistic Goals

It is difficult to fashion social welfare efforts and the system to finance these programs without having an impact upon family life, even though the assumptions made about the effects of the programs may not be spelled out. A major problem underlying recent policies is that governmental interventions fail to pay adequate heed to changing family structure and attitudes about its roles. The basic assumptions concerning the typical American family that prevailed during the 1930s, when many of the current programs were initiated, no longer fit American family life. Furthermore, given the rapid changes that American families are experiencing, grand designs for a new comprehensive family policy are likely to be based on misleading assumptions or values that lack a predominant consensus. Marginal changes in current intervention policies addressed to emerging problems are likely to be more productive.

Both Democratic and Republican administrations in recent years have shown a distinct propensity to oversell their proposals. The Johnson administration promised that the Great Society programs would "open the doors of learning ... rewarding leisure ... and opportunity ... to everyone." The revenue sharing system launched in the early 1970s was far less than the "second American revolution" touted by the Nixon administration. After years of debate, numerous presidential proposals for a unified welfare system have failed to become law. A grand design of family policy is likely to meet a similar fate. While it may be far less dramatic, incremental reform of the already existing system provides the most realistic approach to helping families during this rough period of transition.

Chapter Eight

CASH SUPPORT AND MORE

Each unhappy family is unhappy
in its own way.

Tolstoy, *Anna Karenina*

INCOME SUPPORT

Money may not always be able to buy happiness
and love, as Tolstoy's picture of the wealthy Russian Karenina family
clearly demonstrates. But statistical studies of families often indicate
that lack of adequate financial resources can be a primary cause
behind household dissolution.

The Constitution instructs the federal government to promote the
general welfare. While efforts by the state cannot promise to bring
bliss to all families, government programs can provide basic economic needs and thereby have an impact upon family structure and
behavioral patterns. Since the New Deal, a growing system of cash
support and in-kind aid has been established to help families and
individuals in need. The entire massive transfer payment and in-
kind aid system is not neat and simple. Families with problems
come in all shapes and sizes, and the vastly different household
pathologies defy any one facile formula to provide aid.

Families and Cash Support

Inequality is a problem in all societies at all times.
No system has distributed income evenly, nor necessarily should it.
The reasons for this inequality of income are many. Some are de-

139

sirable and others are unconscionable, but the trends are remarkably constant. Cash income distribution has changed little in recent decades. In 1979 one of every nine American families had an annual cash income of less than $6,000 as follows:

Income Level	Percent
Below $3,000	3%
$3,000–$5,999	8
$6,000–$10,999	17
$11,000–$19,999	30
$20,000 and above	42

In 1980 about one-third of all Americans received assistance from public programs at a price tag in excess of $300 billion, of which four-fifths was paid in cash. Government support programs are the mainstay of the typical poor family, which gets only about two-fifths of its income from wages, salaries, and self-employment (figure 18). Transfer payments, equaling nearly 18 percent of total disposable personal income in 1980, have become a highly significant source

FIGURE 18.

The sources of income are quite different for poor families compared to all households.

Income source

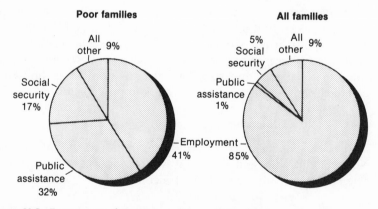

Source: U.S., Department of Commerce, Bureau of the Census

of income for many families—even those who exist well above poverty.

The Social Security Act, the product of more than four decades of evolution since its enactment in 1935, is the most significant public income maintenance program. The law's goal has been to protect families and individuals against the loss of earnings due to specified contingencies in life through two basic groups of programs: (1) social insurance programs—for the aged, the disabled, orphans, and the temporarily unemployed—which distribute payments on the basis of prior earnings and prior tax contribution; and (2) public assistance programs—for the elderly, the blind, the disabled, and families with dependent children—which provide income support on the basis of need alone.

The most comprehensive of the social insurance programs is known as the Old Age, Survivors, and Disability program (OASDI). It is often viewed as mostly tranfer payments to the older population, but about one-third of these OASDI social security checks are sent to people under 65 years of age—including more than 3 million children. One poor family in four receives these benefits. About 95 percent of all children and their mothers would receive benefits if their fathers were to die.

Old age insurance provides income to a steadily rising proportion of the aged population—up to 94 percent in 1980. The elderly accounted for about 20 percent of all the 57 million families and 40 percent of the 20 million nonfamily households. During the 1970s the number of families headed by individuals 65 and over increased 30 percent faster than the total number of households. This increase was due to economic and social changes, as well as demographic shifts. First, the relative number of individuals who live beyond age 64 expanded. Second, broader coverage and payments under the social security system gave many elderly Americans the financial means to run their own households. Accordingly, more and more of them have decided not to live with their children. The role of the extended family was declining even before the social security system was instituted in the United States, but federal insurance and private old age insurance have accelerated this trend.

Declines in the fertility rate have caused concern over the prospect of a vast increase in the ratio of dependent individuals to productive workers. Because OASDI, in effect, transfers income from the working population to the retired generation, some have expressed grave concern that the financial burden on workers will be too great. However, the declining number of children that must be supported could offset the growing number of elderly people. The number of active workers in the labor force per person below age 18 and above age 65 is expected to rise from 1.2 in 1979 to 1.5 in 2010, and then, reflecting the long-range impact of low fertility rates, fall back to 1.2 by about 2035. If this analysis is correct, then it indicates some significant strains on OASDI. But the dependent part of the population (including children) will not be growing unchecked.

When workers retire, their initial benefits are calculated on their covered earnings, averaged over most of their working years, and indexed for inflation. The benefits formula is progressive, with a higher proportion of earnings replacement for lower paid workers. The average monthly payment of about $510 in 1980 for a couple raised many retired workers above the poverty threshold. But benefits remain inadequate to raise some low earners above poverty. In 1979, about 7 percent of cash beneficiaries aged 65 and over also received means-tested welfare Supplemental Security Income payments.

Beyond the problems of the elderly, several basic assumptions built into the system have been increasingly questioned. OASDI was designed to fit the needs of families as they were structured during the late 1930s. The assumption was that in most cases the husband would be employed and the wife would remain at home to care for dependent children and therefore not qualify for social security on the basis of her own earnings. It was also assumed that, once married, a couple would stay together. The equity of these formulas has been questioned, now that a majority of adult women and wives are in the labor force and more marriages end in divorce.

One problem is that a wife's earnings result in higher total family benefits only if her entitlement exceeds the 50 percent spouse's benefit she could receive based on her husband's earnings. In most cases the two-earner couple pays far more into the system than a one-earner couple, but the added contribution and labor results in only minor benefit increases for the two-earner household. Social security payments depend not only upon the amount paid into the system but also on the beneficiaries' household living arrangements. Two people with the same covered earnings can receive far different payments depending upon their household situation.

A few examples illustrate these differences. Consider two couples both of whom have average annual earnings of $12,000. The first couple is a one-earner family and the second is a two-earner family. Despite the same total family average annual earnings, the benefits paid to the one-earner family would be 20 percent greater than those paid to the two-earner couple, because the benefit formula is based on individual earnings. The problem can be even more complicated as this example of a third couple shows. This couple is a two-earner family in which the one member has an average annual earnings of $12,000 and the other, $4,800. The third couple's covered earnings would be 40 percent greater than the first couple's, but their benefits would be only about 3 percent greater. Survivor benefits follow a similar pattern. In fact, the survivor of a two-earner couple in some cases can be paid lower benefits than the surviving spouse of a one-earner couple with the same average annual earnings. Even if the two-earner couple had higher joint earnings, the survivor in many cases will not receive a larger benefit.

Given the current benefits formula and existing conditions within American labor markets, working wives' contributions to the OASDI fund frequently make a very small difference in benefits paid. If the assumption of the one-earner family were dropped, a payment formula could be devised to better reflect married women's significant role in the labor force. But any new formula is likely to increase total outlays, and considering the strapped financial condition of the social security system, Congress is understandably reluctant to raise benefits.

The second problem concerning the equity of the social security system grows out of changes to adjust the initial assumption of lifetime marriages to reflect a growing rate of divorce. Currently, spouse benefits are paid to a worker's divorced wife—if she does not remarry—provided the couple was married for at least 10 years. However, the benefits for such divorcees tend to be small—about half her former husband's benefits. No distinction is made—beyond the ten-year limit—for either the length of the marriage or the wife's age at the time of divorce.

Several possible changes in the system could bring it into better alignment with American family life today. One possibility would be to institute a system of individual benefits and eliminate all dependent and survivor benefits. In conjunction, policies could be instituted to equalize the labor market experiences and household responsibilities between adult men and women; in effect, to equalize both benefits and contributions. This approach, however, would reduce the total benefits paid to couples where one spouse either did not work or earned little. Adoption of this option is, therefore, remote; it probably would produce more losers than winners.

A second option would be to institute homemaker credits for women who remain full-time housewives. These homemaker credits would be determined arbitrarily, and benefits would be paid without reference to need and would thus be tantamount to a grant. As this approach would increase the benefits paid out, but not the contributions paid in, it could be hard to fund at a time when the social security system faces difficult financial decisions. The political reality is that in order to get the homemaker credit adopted, it would have to be made so small that it would provide only marginal benefits. At the same time, a homemaker credit would not alter the problems of the one-earner versus the two-earner couple.

A third way to adjust the system would be earnings-sharing programs. One form of earnings-sharing might be to award benefits to couples as individuals based on their own shared records. Besides providing greater protection to divorced homemakers, earnings-sharing could equalize the benefits paid to one-earner and two-earner couples. As Nancy M. Gordon has noted, under earnings-sharing social security records would become "another monetary asset accumulated during marriage," and the shared records would, in effect, resemble joint property owned by both partners. However, earnings-sharing would add to the costs of the system unless benefits paid to primary beneficiaries were cut.[1]

On balance, the achievements of the social security system overshadow any inequities, real or apparent. The system has helped numerous families in what otherwise would have been difficult times. It has provided surviving beneficiaries, as well as older Americans, needed resources to remain financially independent and to maintain their own households. Nevertheless, this does not mean that the benefit and contribution formulas should be rigid and not adjusted to reflect changes in American living patterns. Earnings-sharing adjustments or a combination of the options indicated above could be phased in over time without causing undue stress on the system, so that it would better reflect the record numbers of women in the labor force. Even with shifts in American household structure, the underlying objectives of the system make just as much sense today as they did when the act was passed in 1935.

Public Assistance

The Social Security Act also provides means-tested aid to families. By far the largest, costliest, and most controversial public assistance program is Aid to Families with Dependent Children (AFDC). Assistance is also provided to the aged, blind, and disabled through the Supplemental Security Income (SSI) program.

AFDC is identified with "welfare" because it has accounted for most of the increase in means-tested income support since World War II. Despite these programs, over half of the families that receive public assistance income remain poor.

In 1980, there were over 10 million AFDC recipients, including 7.2 million children, or one of every nine children. Direct care payments during 1979 totaled $12 billion. Though the federal government contributed more than half of the total cost for AFDC, it delegates administration of the programs to the states, within broad federal guidelines. Most important, the states determine eligibility standards and the level of benefits. The grant paid to the recipient is based on need standards determined by each state, and varies widely among the states. The standard nominally reflects minimal cost of rent, utilities, food, clothing, and other basic expenses. In many states, however, there is little correlation between actual living costs and established need standards. As of January 1980, monthly payments per family averaged $272, or $93 per individual recipient, and ranged from lows of $88 in Mississippi and $109 in Texas to $386 in Hawaii and $398 in Rhode Island.

Fathers are "officially" present in only one AFDC home in nine, and over half of these men are disabled. Nearly half of the AFDC families are nonwhite. AFDC mothers have substantially lower educational attainment than other women of the same age level, and their work experience also has serious limitations. Almost one-fourth have never been employed and, of those who have worked, one-fourth worked in private households or other employment that generally provides meager earnings.

Since World War II, AFDC has grown phenomenally, doubling the number of beneficiaries each decade between 1947 and 1967 and again between 1967 and 1972, when the expansion virtually ceased (except for a mild increase during the recession in the mid-1970s), as the bulk of needy female-headed families qualified for assistance. The reasons for the expansion of AFDC are many and complex. Not only did more people become eligible, but also benefits were increased and the stigma attached to welfare was reduced.

Population growth, especially among children, contributed significantly to swelling the AFDC rolls. But perhaps more important was the increasing number of households headed by women who are potential AFDC recipients. AFDC may be viewed as a response to economic and social pressures resulting from the rise of the single-parent family, but the program itself may induce families to modify their behavior in order to qualify for benefits. AFDC may encourage the very phenomenon to which it is a response, by inducing a couple to beget children without getting married. It also may offer an incentive for an unemployed man to desert his family so that his dependents can be eligible for assistance in the 23 states where families with unemployed fathers are ineligible for public assistance. Some critics have gone as far as to say that because of these negative impacts on families, welfare is doing more harm than good. Yet the data on these tough issues are far from unequivocal.

The evidence that the greater availability of welfare has reduced the propensity to marry even after conception is mostly anecdotal.[2] Charges that mothers on welfare have additional children in order to qualify for higher payments remain unsubstantiated. A married woman who becomes a family head can expect a substantial drop in her level of economic well-being—even with public assistance factored into the family budget equation.[3] Finally, most of the increase in the number of female-headed households is accounted for by childless women who are ineligible for public assistance benefits.

Federal legislation and Supreme Court decisions have added to the welfare population by extending coverage to groups who were not previously eligible. In 1961, Congress allowed states to extend eligibility for AFDC assistance to families with an unemployed—but employable—parent and 27 states have taken advantage of this provision. In 1968, the court struck down the "man in the house" rule, which held that a man living in an AFDC house was responsible for the children's support even if he was not legally liable. The following year, the Supreme Court invalidated residency requirements for public assistance. Income disregards—whereby states ignore certain earnings in determining eligibility payments—have permitted many families, who would otherwise have been disqualified, to enter or remain on the rolls.

A basic condition for the growth was the broader attractiveness of AFDC relative to other income sources. Although AFDC cash payments trailed rises in cost of living during the 1970s, significant expansion in corollary programs—the provision of food stamps, free school lunches, subsidized housing, medicaid, and social services—tilted the economic balance so that many families favored welfare over poorly paid jobs.

On the other hand, these developments apparently complicated the choice between work and welfare for many families, as the widespread incidence of supplementing earnings from work with welfare suggests. Almost three of five families receiving AFDC also have some labor market earnings. A breadwinner with three dependents in a state that pays high welfare benefits, such as Rhode Island or California, would need a full-time job paying more than $4.25 an hour (in 1979 dollars) to match the value of combined cash support, food stamp grants, and other in-kind assistance for a four-member family.

The preceding summary does not disprove the charges that AFDC has disrupted marital and family patterns, especially among minorities. Economic factors, however, explain only a part of the changes in marital and family patterns; welfare is only one of these economic factors. Statistical models that include only a few independent variables show some AFDC impact on families, but models that include nonwelfare related variables show a much smaller AFDC impact— so little in many cases that it is not significant.

Work and Family Welfare

Back in the 1930s, the AFDC program was viewed as aid to destitute widows who needed financial support in raising children. The female family head was not expected to work, but to be fully occupied in rearing her children. Labor market conditions also were not conducive to encouraging mothers to work outside their homes; there was a shortage of jobs even for married men, who were seen as more deserving of employment. Moreover, the social mores of the times did not encourage mothers with young children to become wage earners.

As time passed, the picture changed. The AFDC mother was often not a widow, and in many cases she had never been married. Also, the number and proportion of nonwhite mothers on AFDC vastly increased. Meanwhile, the social norms regarding women in the labor force changed significantly. As more mothers (even those with very young children) entered the work force, a growing number of critics argued that welfare mothers should earn their living.

Prior to 1967, the benefits paid under AFDC were most often calculated as the difference between a client's own income and the maximum payment standard established by a state, although minimal work expenses were allowed. Hence, benefits would be reduced by whatever amount the family head earned. This "marginal tax rate," or benefit reduction of 100 percent, created a disincentive to work. To overcome this disincentive, Congress in 1967 created the Work Incentive (WIN) program, which established the formula of "$30 + ⅓ + Work Expenses." Under this formula, welfare officials were required to disregard the first $30 plus one-third of the remaining monthly wages and work-related expenses in computing benefits, even if this brought a family's total income (earnings combined with welfare) above a state's needs standard. This was viewed as inducement to get AFDC family heads into the labor force. Yet the earnings level required—assuming jobs were available—to remove a family of four from AFDC is more than many AFDC mothers can command.

To complement WIN, tax credits have been legislated to induce private employers to hire welfare recipients. Despite their theoretical appeal, these tax credits have achieved little so far to relieve welfare rolls. The reported national average rate of employment among AFDC mothers remains fairly stable despite WIN and other provisions.

In recent years successive administrations have proposed major changes of the welfare system. While the plans differed, their common goal was to assure a minimal income to families with children and to induce adults in these families to work. The Carter administration proposed a system designed to stimulate welfare recipients' work efforts through massive public job creation efforts. While the words "income guarantee" were not used, under the Carter proposal all destitute families with children would have been eligible to receive a basic level of federal cash aid equal to 65 percent of the poverty threshold. Beyond this amount, those who did work would have wound up receiving more income at jobs paying the minimum wage. However, Congress rejected the proposed basic reforms in the welfare system; conservatives opposed the plans as being too costly and liberals felt that the proposals did not provide adequate guaranteed income. Whatever the underlying objections, Congress was reluctant to commit added billions to welfare outlays regardless of the promised reform that might result.

There are three basic strategies to replace or reform the existing welfare system: (1) either a guaranteed income or negative income tax; (2) child allowances; and (3) employment guarantees or wage subsidies. These approaches are not mutually exclusive and can be combined in a total package. While all three paths contain some benefits for improving family welfare, they also involve added costs and other drawbacks.

A negative income tax could, for example, guarantee a family of four an income equal to the poverty threshold (i.e., $7,400 in 1979 dollars). If a family with four members had an annual income of, say, $4,000, then they would receive a grant equaling $3,400. However, guaranteeing a poverty-level income would be expensive. Also, it might reduce the pecuniary incentives to work for millions of families, because their incomes would remain at the poverty threshold whether or not they held jobs. To counter this possibility, any workable plan must allow low-wage workers to keep at least a portion of their earned income. For example, half the earnings of low-income families might be exempt. Thus a family of four with an income of $4,000 would count only $2,000 for tax purposes and would be able to claim $5,500 for a total income of $9,500, compared with the $7,400 maximum paid to a family without a wage earner.

Finding consensus on a formula for a negative income tax has proven to be quite difficult. If the guarantee is set too low, it will leave many families and individuals in dire economic hardship. If it is set too high, then many families significantly above poverty will be able to claim benefits. Yet incentives must be attractive enough to induce able-bodied workers to contribute to their family's support. A low tax rate is of no help to those who cannot work, while a high benefit level may draw able-bodied workers out of the labor market. Combining a high benefit level with a low tax rate would qualify many middle-income families. Ever present as a constraint on benefits and incentives is the cost of such a program.

Despite these problems, public policy is moving in the direction of some form of a guaranteed income. Currently, given the wage structure and other labor market features, the number of households on welfare that can achieve total independence through employment is quite low. A realistic program would view work as complementing welfare and not force recipients to choose either work or welfare. The underlying justification would be the recognition that millions of Americans will remain among the working poor—even if they can find and keep a steady job.

Another method of providing cash assistance is to pay families with children an allowance to supplement their own income to meet some portion of the costs of childbearing. This proposal recognizes that the wage system alone distributes income inadequately, because wages are based on productivity or tradition rather than on need. The underlying justification for family allowances is that a child's well-being should concern society as a whole.

The United States, as noted, is the only advanced industrialized nation without a family allowance program. Except for adjustments in income tax deductions, the take-home pay for a bachelor is often the same as for the head of a family with dependents in an identical job. The armed forces are unique in having traditionally adjusted compensation based on the number of dependents. In some countries all children are eligible for subsidies, while in others no benefits are paid for the first or second child. Benefits are usually paid for children up to the age they would normally leave school, but they may be extended for further schooling, training, or apprenticeship. The allowance per child may also vary. For example, France has a complex system that adjusts for family income and size and for children's ages.[4]

Family allowance programs are not a complete alternative to a guaranteed income because many people living in poverty do not have children. Because a means test is not needed for a family allowance system, the plan would greatly reduce administrative costs and would interfere relatively little with work incentives. Also, a program that would give benefits to all children probably would find broader political support than any other alternative. On the other hand, the potential cost of a universal family allowance might lead politicians to settle on such small level of benefits that the system would have only a very marginal effect on families.

Less heralded than the guaranteed income plans are proposals to guarantee employment and to subsidize wages. A "family wage" could alter the payments to a worker depending upon the individual's family responsibilities. In part, the tax system does recognize these differences through deductions and exemptions. However, the principle of rewarding each worker on the basis of family needs has gained little support.

Other programs such as unemployment insurance, general assistance, workers' compensation, and, of course, private pensions are all part of a system designed to mitigate many different pathologies and social needs. The entire system is far from unified or simple, and it does not satisfy advocates of a comprehensive and integrated plan. But each program helps households cope with difficulties they encounter, and 12 states provide added unemployment benefits for dependents.

IN-KIND AID

It has been argued that a negative income tax, a family allowance system, and other cash support programs could replace in-kind goods and services provided to needy households by the government. However, families in need require in-kind goods and services as well as cash support. The view that all in-kind aid can be "cashed out" rests on several highly questionable claims. In many cases it is unrealistic to expect that the private sector will provide these essential goods and services even if families are given added cash support. For many reasons poor families face numerous handicaps, or roadblocks, in purchasing essential goods and services from private suppliers. A realistic public policy must include both cash support and in-kind aid.

Since the 1960s Great Society, the government has increased greatly the in-kind goods and services provided for households. While the provision of goods and services accounted for only one-fifth of the federal outlays to poor households in 1964, it accounted for roughly three-fifths by 1980 (figure 19). The growing reliance on providing goods and services can be traced, in part, to a longstanding public skepticism concerning the moral character and reliability of poor households. The fear is that if only cash support were given, the funds would not be used to purchase such basic items as food, shelter, and medical care. But because of the isolation of some needy families and shortcomings in the market mechanism, it has been recognized that more than cash is required. It is doubtful that all of

FIGURE 19.

In-kind assistance to households has grown much faster than cash support (1979 dollars).

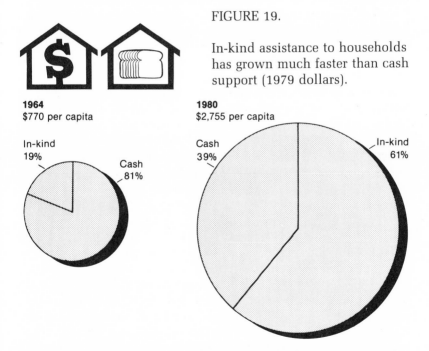

1964
$770 per capita

In-kind 19%

Cash 81%

1980
$2,755 per capita

Cash 39%

In-kind 61%

Source: U.S., Department of Commerce; authors' estimates for 1980 based on earlier estimates by Gordon Fisher, *Statistical Abstracts of the United States* (Washington, D.C.: Government Printing Office, 1975), p. 405.

these services would be provided to needy families by the private suppliers without some government efforts in these areas.

The Next Generation

Beyond coping with existing family related difficulties, several government programs have aimed at preventing such problems. Assisting couples in keeping family size within their desires and means will aid the next generation to begin at less of a disadvantage. Providing care to preschool children can alleviate some family pressures and help family heads—and potential second wage earners—enter the labor force. Policies regarding education can have a significant impact on family life.

Not only has there been a marked increase in the number of adults who use some form of birth control, but the types of methods they use have changed and improved in quality. The laws associated with birth control have also changed. In 1973 the Supreme Court struck down restrictive state laws regarding abortion, especially during the first three months of pregnancy.

National opinion research indicates vast changes in attitudes toward abortion. In 1968, about seven of eight adults opposed abortions based solely on the desire not to have another child, but by the end of the 1970s only one of two adults felt this way. Similarly, the percentage of adult Americans who believed that birth control information should be available to anyone who wants it rose from 73 in 1959 to over 90 at the end of the 1970s. The largest change in attitudes on this matter has occurred among Catholics: between 1964 and 1977, the proportion of Catholics favoring the distribution of birth control rose from three of five to roughly six of seven.[5]

Changes in birth control technology and law notwithstanding, unwanted and unplanned births remain a too frequent occurrence. The incidence of unwanted births is greater for lower income and poorly educated households. A woman with a college degree has only about an 8 percent chance of having an unwanted birth, but for women who have not completed a high school education this chance increases to roughly 33 percent.[6] The evidence is clear that limited access to birth control devices and family planning services has deprived many women unable to afford medical care of the same degree of choice open to more affluent women.

About 10 percent of all females between the ages of 15 and 19 become pregnant annually, accounting for close to 600,000 births per year. Of this total, more than three of seven are born out of wedlock. There is ample evidence that a teenage single mother is going to face many difficult problems. In many cases, both mother and child end up on welfare. Teenagers account for more than a quarter-million AFDC mothers. Even if teenage parents do marry and support their offspring, their education is still likely to be interrupted and their job opportunities may be limited for life. There is also considerable evidence that early parenthood leads to larger families, placing continuing economic burdens upon the household.[7]

About 6.5 million poor and near-poor women were in need of organized family planning services in 1980. The cost of providing a patient with a gynecological examination and birth control devices was about $90 a year. A comprehensive program to furnish services would cost about $600 million annually, and the federal government contributed about a fourth of the needed funds. While funding in the area increased dramatically during the late 1960s and 1970s, it did not meet total potential demand. Inadequacy of funds is endemic to social programs, but appears less justified in case of birth control efforts whose cost effectiveness is well proven. The increasing support of federal legislation with the goal of providing family planning services to all women who need and desire them reflects the expanded consensus that fertility control is not only a valuable contribution to family life but also an effective measure in preventing poverty. Accordingly, all states participating in Medicaid are required to provide such services. The goal is to expand services in areas with high teenage birth rates.

The number of women served by organized programs rose from less than 900,000 in 1968 to more than 4.3 million a decade later (figure 20). Roughly three of every four clients had incomes of less than 150 percent of the poverty level. An additional 1.6 million low-income women received family planning service from private physicians. Despite the rapid expansion of federal family planning services, about 30 percent of eligible low-income women of childbearing age receive no subsidized family planning services. Public assistance recipients made up one-fifth of the women served by ongoing programs and those served accounted for about one-fourth of eligible women assisted by public welfare. Related to family planning, although not necessarily tied to it, is the issue of abortion. Many who favor federal support for family planning are opposed to abortion.

Federal support of child care has remained an important political issue. Most child care arrangements are informal, either in the child's or the caretaker's home, although the number of licensed child care centers and nursery schools almost quadrupled during the 1960s and 1970s. About 6 million children aged 3 to 5 now participate in

FIGURE 20.

The number of patients receiving organized family planning services has increased vastly since 1968.

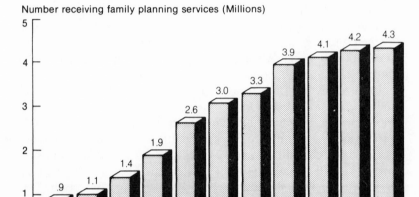

Number receiving family planning services (Millions)

Source: Aida Torres, "Organized Family Planning Services in the United States," *Perspectives* (November/December 1979), p. 342; unpublished data from the Alan Guttmacher Institute.

some form of school or formal out-of-home child care program.[8] Government efforts and support have had a major influence in this growth. Toward the end of the 1970s, the federal government contributed over $2 billion for the purchase of about 1.5 million years of child care through programs supporting welfare clients and other near-poor persons. When direct programs are included the number of children whose care is subsidized reaches over 5 million.[9]

In addition to direct subsidies, a limited tax deduction for work-related child care expenses has been available since 1954. The law has been liberalized, allowing increasing proportions of middle- and upper-income families to take advantage of the provision. Families with an annual income below $35,000 may deduct expenses up to a maximum of $4,800 a year, a figure that is reduced 50 cents for every dollar of income over $35,000. In 1978, a tax credit was allowed for child care payments to nondependent relatives.

There is growing evidence that child care combined with early education not only frees mothers to work outside the home but also helps improve the future school record of children from poor families. While expansion of child care combined with teaching ABCs entails considerable costs, low fertility rates will help contain these outlays. As the number of school-age youngsters falls, many local areas would be able to provide preschool facilities without a massive investment in plant and equipment. Child care would be a realistic use of some of the currently idle educational resources. Also, in a welfare state the alternative costs that must be paid for *not* providing child care services must be considered.

To maintain separate facilities for children of working mothers tends to segregate these children, especially if eligibility for enrollment is based on low income. To help working mothers, child care that would supplement expanded school programs rather than compete with them is a preferable alternative to segregated systems. The added school facilities could be open to all children in keeping with the traditional practice of serving children from all classes. Federal guidelines and monitoring would be required to assure that the needs of children from low-income families are not ignored in a universal system. Child care facilities remain relatively scarce, and proposals in this area remain high on the agenda of almost all family policy advocates.

Expanding Services

Beyond programs for the next generation, in-kind aid has vastly reduced economic hardship by helping families meet their basic needs for health care, food, and shelter. However, shifting family conditions have affected several basic assumptions contained in these programs.

Under the current concept of the welfare state, a basic minimum level of medical treatment is in theory viewed as a right not dependent upon the financial condition of an individual family. Since the passage of Medicare and Medicaid in 1965, the federal government has assumed the major responsibility as the provider of health care for the aged and the poor. Despite massive public expenditures (more than $16 billion in 1980), the deficit in health care remains startling, whether measured in life expectancy, infant mortality rate, or numbers of visits to physicians or dentists. In general, adults and children in husband-wife families experience fewer health problems than individuals in other household structures when the data are adjusted for differences including race, age, and other variables. However, it is not clear that a true cause-and-effect relationship exists between health problems and family structure. It could be, for example, that single-parent families have more health-related problems because they tend to have lower incomes than two-adult families. Or, it could be that medical problems are a prime cause of family dissolution, which creates the single-parent family. Whatever the path of causation, a higher proportion of children and adults in broken families have serious medical problems—and they have fewer resources to cope with these difficulties. This is particularly true for households headed by elderly individuals.

Medicare covers the bulk of hospital and medical costs of persons who are 65 years of age and older and disabled social security beneficiaries. All social security and railroad retirement recipients and others who meet special qualifications are entitled to Medicare hospital insurance, which in 1980 covered about 27 million persons, and roughly 6.5 million of these received hospital care. Medicare provisions have helped a growing number of elderly Americans maintain their own households. It is a universal program designed to help the elderly regardless of their income. No doubt Medicare has kept many near-poor elderly out of poverty, and it has eased the anxieties of those elderly whose life savings would have been wiped out by a major illness.

Medicaid was launched in 1965 to replace a fragmented system of medical assistance to beneficiaries of separate public assistance programs. It offers reimbursement to states for a portion of the medical costs of low-income households; the federal share of expenses range from 50 to 78 percent, dependent upon the scope of services provided and eligibility requirements. Each state administers and operates its own programs, setting its own rules within the confines of federal guidelines and regulations. Congress restricted Medicaid to families with an income of no more than one-third above the AFDC income cutoff—a step taken because several states had set significantly higher income ceilings. In 1978 the ceilings ranged from $2,400 to $6,600 for a family of four. Great Society programs also funded community health facilities in an effort to restructure health care systems in poor and rural areas.

Despite these efforts, expanding medical services remains a key part of programs favoring expansion of family policy. With rising medical costs, many families could face serious financial difficulties if one of their members required hospitalization. Policymakers so far have not been able to establish a system to expand these efforts. While a nationalized medical system—similar to the United Kingdom's—is rejected by many analysts, there are other policies that could promote family stability. For example, universal comprehensive insurance against serious medical risks is one option. This type of universal insurance could be geared to provide nationally established minimum standards of benefits, with periodic upward readjustments reflecting changes in real incomes, medical costs, technology, and social standards.[10]

The provision of food to low-income households has been another major expanding commitment of the federal government. While the federal food stamp program was in operation nationally from 1939 to 1943, the program was not revived until 1961. Similarly, the diverse child nutrition programs were not launched until the Great Society era of the 1960s with the creation of the school lunch, school breakfast, and special milk programs. After a slow beginning on these food programs in the 1960s, the following decade witnessed a massive growth in federal spending for direct food assistance, reaching almost $13 billion by 1980.

Over 90 percent of all benefits under these food programs are distributed on the basis of need, and perhaps more than in any other in-kind aid program destitute households receive an overwhelming share of this federal assistance. In 1980, nearly 20 million persons received monthly allotments of food stamps based on their household's income and size. The stamps can be exchanged in retail stores for food. The maximum monthly food stamp allotment for a family of four was $209. This amount is reduced based on the family's income. A family of four with a monthly income of $500 was entitled to receive $82 in food stamps. Benefit levels are adjusted periodically to reflect changes in food prices.

The expansion of the program has reflected wider eligibility for benefits, more generous formulas for calculating benefits, and higher unemployment rates in recent years. More than three of five households that receive food stamps are headed by a female, and one of five food stamp households contain a person who is age 65 or over. Participation in the program varies with a household's public assistance status. In 1977, more than 90 percent of the public assistance households eligible for the program received food stamps, but only half of the other eligible nonpublic assistance households participated in the program.[11]

Families with children are much more likely to participate in the program than households in the same economic conditions that do not have any youngsters. Permanently disabled heads of households also show very high participation rates in the food stamp program. The program also remains one of the few federal initiatives that extends help to family heads who are active members of the labor force but remain part of the working poor, although 60 percent of household heads receiving food stamps are not in the labor force.[12]

Allocations for shelter also have represented a major federal effort to help families. The government's efforts include federal mortgage guarantees, loans, subsidies, tax credits, and public housing. The income tax deductions for interest payments on mortgages and for property taxes have helped many middle-income families own homes. In 1940, 44 percent of the nation's dwelling units were owner occupied, compared with some 67 percent currently. Declining fertility rates have shifted demand toward smaller units, and rising divorce rates have reduced the proportion of families that are able to purchase their own units. Massive price increases and rising interest rates have also dampened home purchases.

Few markets are as sensitive to changes in American family patterns as housing.[13] Part of the influx of married women into the labor force appears to be due to stiff financial requirements for home buyers. As these pressures mount—and as the home-buying power of Americans declines—these trends will continue to foster growth in the number of multi–pay check families.

Single-parent families are much more likely to be renters, and only a small portion of the families that experience a divorce are able to hold onto their home. Delinquency and foreclosure rates also indicate that female-headed families tend to face more shelter-related problems than other types of households.[14] The share of total income allocated to shelter is inversely related to the level of a family's income. For divorced women, the share of family income devoted to housing rises from an average 14 percent when married to 27 percent after the divorce; for separated women, the comparable figures are 17 percent and 37 percent. Maintenance expenses have become an extremely difficult burden.[15] Government policies regarding shelter will have to be adjusted to take into consideration the changes in American household patterns.

As federal programs helping poor families expanded during the 1960s, Congress increasingly acknowledged the importance of social services in helping families. The scope of social services is so broad that they almost defy definition; they range from specifics, such as child and foster care, drug and alcohol abuse treatment, and legal aid, to general forms of assistance, such as counseling or programs designed to strengthen family life.

If the content of social services is somewhat amorphous, the cost certainly is not. Under a 1967 law authorizing open-ended federal matching funds (3 federal dollars for every state dollar) for social services to former, current, or potential welfare recipients, state requests for federal funds quickly ballooned to over $4 billion by 1972. The congressional response to burgeoning program costs set an annual ceiling on federal expenditures; the cap was $2.9 billion in 1979. This ceiling has held growth rates for social service costs well below those for other federal in-kind assistance programs. Congress has also restricted free services to families whose income is below either the national median or 80 percent of the state's median income.

Other congressional initiatives have emphasized family planning services for the poor by raising federal matching grants for this purpose from 75 to 90 percent. Programs have been targeted to provide child care services and child welfare services designed to keep low-income families together and enable adults in the family to work. While such efforts can be viewed as long-range investments and alternatives to costly cash and in-kind assistance programs, the federal commitment to social services is certain to lag far behind the massive outlays for the daily necessities of needy families in the future.

POLICY CONSTRAINTS

While government policy should not be used to enforce one rigid type of family structure, its efforts can have a beneficial impact. It is best that government policy focus on providing the necessary resources to prevent the birth of unwanted children. But public policy should ensure that all children, once born, receive a basic standard of living regardless of the household structure in which they live. Public policy is moving slowly in this direction. Cash support programs have been expanded in a majority of states to include aid if there is an unemployed parent. Beyond this more limited support, American policy is moving in the direction of income guarantees for families with children.

A comprehensive and grand family policy may look tempting, but it is not the best road down which to travel. Besides real budget constraints, many Americans will continue to resist having their family life being fitted to any one procrustean bed.

Full employment, a man on the moon, energy independence—all may serve as slogans and objectives in other fields, but there is no similar rallying cry in family matters. It is appealing to favor a stronger American family, but what does this mean? Does this mean making it very difficult to obtain a divorce, outlawing abortion, reinstating prayer in public schools, installing a full-time wife in the home, and boosting the average number of children per family? Others would view a stronger family as one having equal partners, no roadblocks to obtaining a divorce and starting over, or even the right of homosexuals to marry and adopt children.

In essence, public policy can be used to ease the transition and buffetting American families are experiencing. But public policy will not be able—nor should it attempt—to "fine tune" families into fitting any one paradigm or norm.

Chapter Nine

CHANGING INSTITUTIONS AND FINANCIAL ARRANGEMENTS

> My lofty ideals—which I now have well under
> control—prevented me from seeing the workings of the
> social machinery; I was compelled to see it in the end
> by bumping against its wheels, knocking into its shaft,
> getting covered with its grease, and hearing the constant
> clatter of its chains and fly-wheels.
>
> Honoré de Balzac, *Lost Illusions*

WORKING FOR ADJUSTMENTS

After several unsuccessful efforts to change what he viewed as hypocritical Parisian customs, Balzac's young hero, Lucien, is eloquently told that he cannot fight city hall. Lucien heeds this advice given by an older friend, and by the end of the story he not only has conformed to the social institutions of the day but also has learned how to turn them cynically to his own advantage. Despite bumping into the wheels and knocking into the shafts, millions of Americans have not given up on basic efforts to alter the social machinery that affects family life.

Beyond public assistance or in-kind aid, family policies must explore the workings of other basic institutions. How labor markets function, or fail to function, can have a strong influence on families. The courts and the tax system also have a major impact on family life. The interrelationships between outside institutions and the home have been increasingly called into question.

Labor Markets

Millions of family heads fail, or are being failed, in labor markets. Lack of work is an obvious reason, but finding a job is no guarantee that it will pay enough to raise the worker and his or her family out of poverty. Altogether, some 2.5 million heads of families who work during a year remain in destitution, and these include nearly 1 million who work at full-time, full-year jobs. Almost one-quarter of female family heads have strong labor force attachment, earn less than the poverty line, and live in households that have family incomes less than twice the poverty threshold. More than 8 percent of all husband-wife families experience similar economic hardship.[1]

Besides unemployment and low wages, discrimination has been a major cause of hardship among families headed by females, blacks, Hispanics, and other minority groups. Title VII of the Civil Rights Act of 1964 and a series of other laws have sought to ban discriminatory employment practices. However, significant wage and promotion differences based on sex and race persist, even when data are adjusted to consider other variables such as employment in part-time jobs. Like inequality in household responsibilities, discrimination in the labor market remains very real. This has a serious negative impact on the earnings ability of female- and minority-headed families.

Family environment has a significant impact on the types of remedial training required and the outcomes of specific programs. It is difficult to counteract in a 6-month training course the influence ° living, say, 18 years in a neglectful household, and the human urce investment may be too little and too late, or have only a ¬al effect. Given the recent structural shifts in American family ¬reater attention will have to be given to the earlier years of ¹ual's development and his or her household living con- ¬ay be that greater returns would be obtained if more ¬ allocated for career education and training prior to ¬individuals are expected to support themselves or ¬ilies.

¬d apparently has a very strong influence on ¬tudy estimated that almost half the occupa- ¬e-fifths of the earnings advantage of people ¬g jobs, appear to be due to their family the laws of supply and demand and ¹s are highly cognizant of an individ-

╵ failed or are being failed in the

labor market, the government has sponsored a number of employment and training programs. Since 1973 many of these efforts have been consolidated under the Comprehensive Employment and Training Act (CETA). Since the passage of the act, Congress has increasingly limited eligibility for CETA assistance to unemployed members of low-income families. All persons eligible for welfare are automatically eligible for CETA-funded services. In 1979 more than 40 percent of CETA-funded public service employment positions were held by family heads and 30 percent of enrollees had two or more dependents when they entered employment and training programs. More than four of five CETA job recipients have family incomes at or below the poverty level or are otherwise eligible for public assistance.[3]

The Work Incentive (WIN) program is a related government effort designed to help members of families receiving public assistance. WIN began by promising needed comprehensive services to each enrollee. Because enrollees often need basic education and skill training as well as child care and other supportive services, success has been modest. While the program may have helped some enrollees to leave the rolls, it is impossible that it will lower welfare costs or provide a permanent exit from poverty and dependence.

American society appears still to place a high value on the work ethic, but seems willing to pay only a low price for fostering it. More than 6 million adults were employed at or below the minimum wage, which stood at $3.10 an hour in 1980. Without a wage floor that is kept in line with changing price levels and growth in productivity, the income gained from welfare could outpace the rewards obtained from work for millions of families. Welfare could then become an increasingly rational alternative to work for a growing number of households. For these reasons a minimum wage is needed as a floor to express the socially recognized value of labor rather than just to meet income needs. Edward Gramlich concluded that female workers are a group that needs labor market protection, and they may be helped the most by the wage floor.[4] Family policies in a welfare state that try to encourage more household members to enter the labor force will require an active wage floor. Current proposals to exempt workers from minimum wage coverage may result in swelling welfare rolls.

Alternative Work Schedules

Rigid work schedules remain an obstacle to married women and single family heads who are seeking jobs, and inflexible work schedules can create strains on mothers who find employment.

As many working wives have discovered, a majority of women do not exchange the role of housewife for paid worker. Instead, they are expected to fill two jobs. Or, as one TV jingle advertised:

> I can put the wash on the line, feed the kids
> Get dressed, pass out the kisses
> And get to work by five to nine
> Cause I'm a wo-man.

Instead of the older norm of a woman's role, a new "Superwoman" or "High Powered Mom" cult has developed in which a woman is expected to be a tireless temptress for the man, or men, in her life, a devoted mother for her children, a human dynamo on the job, and a perfect housekeeper. This new vision is, in many ways, harder to live up to than the older, and simpler, standard. It is quite difficult for many women, including female family heads, to fit into the standard 40-hour workweek. Alternatives to the worktime rigidities, including flexible work schedules and worksharing, would make it easier for more women to have productive and sane lives both on the job and at home. Such policies would recognize the unique problems many female workers face meeting household responsibilities and job-related demands. It could also ease the transition experienced by families as either a wife or a female family head enters the labor force.

Some adjustments in creating part-time work have been made in recent years to accommodate the needs of women with family responsibilities and youngsters going to school. In 1980 about 30 percent of the workers labored fewer than 40 hours per week, compared with 17 percent in 1948. Yet more than 40 percent of the persons employed in the United States still worked exactly 40 hours per week. There has been some reduction in the proportion of people putting in workweeks longer than 40 hours, but the 40-hour workweek for full-time workers has remained remarkably constant since World War II.

About 17 million people worked on part-time schedules (1 to 34 hours per week) in 1980, or one of every six people in the labor force. Almost three-fourths of these worked short hours because they did not want, or were unavailable for, full-time jobs. The others were on reduced work schedules for economic reasons such as slack work or inability to find a full-time job. Women represented nearly 70 percent of the more than 13 million voluntary part-time workers; up from 65 percent in 1965. In fact, wives accounted for the majority of workers laboring fewer than 35 hours per week.

While many wives may seek part-time employment, female family heads who work tend to seek full-time jobs. More than three of five working female family heads hold down full-time positions. Alternative and flexible work schedules can be designed to help more women meet the multiple demands of being a wage earner, mother, and wife, or single parent. These different work patterns can take various forms. For example, an employer can establish a core period of working hours, say in the middle of the working day, when workers must be on the job. Then workers would have the option of picking either periods in the morning, afternoon, or evening to make up the rest of their scheduled hours. Despite the growing number of employers who have started "flexitime" programs, alternative work schedules remain the exception rather than the rule in America.

The data and evidence are still too scanty to draw lasting conclusions, but it does appear that many working mothers are helped by these programs. When given a chance, many workers opt for flexitime systems.[5] Flexitime is widespread in several European nations. However, only one of six American employers has used some form of a rearranged workweek.[6]

An alternative to flexitime is jobsharing, whereby work schedules remain rigid but a single job is shared by, say, two persons each working half-time. In addition, worksharing sometimes is used as an alternative to layoffs. In 1979, it is estimated that only about 1.6 million workers were worksharers, and close to half of them were women.[7] Worksharing could operate in the following way. If a firm must reduce the total hours worked by, say, 30 percent during an economic slump, it can turn to the layoff system and 30 percent of its work force would be unemployed. Or, the firm can use worksharing to reduce the workweek for all of its employees by 30 percent. Workers would then be compensated for a part of the wages lost due to reduced hours through some system such as unemployment insurance. A major benefit of worksharing is that employment gains made by minority and women workers are not lost during a recession, whereas such workers are most often the first to be fired under a layoff system.

While worksharing and flexitime may produce benefits for society and individual families, these plans also carry a cost. From the employer's standpoint, instituting alternative work schedules is often more expensive than using more standard methods of adjusting total hours (i.e., layoffs to reduce hours or overtime to increase them). This is true because rising overtime may hold down expenditures for fringe benefits and other fixed labor costs. Also, some union officials have indicated concern that flexitime systems will be used to undermine the gains they have won under collective bargaining.[8]

The interrelationship between families and the labor market indicates that these issues regarding worktime will not go away. Many of the forces that have propped up worktime since World War II are now shifting in the opposite direction. The postwar baby boom, combined with the increasing costs of rearing children and a persistent yearning for a rising standard of living, has induced many households to trade potential gains in leisure for more income. The recent high rates of inflation have reinforced the preference for more money over more leisure in an effort just to keep real family income constant. Analyses that take into account changes in the number of children and the costs of rearing them, the level of schooling, and rates of inflation can explain why the workweek has not dropped dramatically during the last 40 years.[9]

However, some of these very same forces—especially lower birth rates—are now exerting far different influences and can be expected to continue in the same vein in the near future. As Juanita Kreps has noted, the growth in married women's labor force participation rates could tilt the family's leisure-income trade-off in the direction of leisure, because a good portion of the time that economists tend to call "leisure" really is spent on household work.[10] Such a tilt in the income-leisure decision probably will not be a massive swing of the pendulum, but even a small change can have an important cumulative impact. Because of the changing composition of the labor force, more workers are likely to prefer shorter hours.

Labor markets should be able to accommodate some of these preferences. Employment growth in the service sector, which has used a major proportion of part-time workers, including wives, should be increasing faster than in the economy as a whole. But government intervention also may be necessary. The wider introduction of flexitime and worksharing will require federal policies that reduce the costs of following these alternatives. One example would be changes in the rules regarding unemployment insurance so that it can be used for worksharing compensation, as California has already done on a modest scale.

Maternity leaves are also a problem for many working women and their families. As noted earlier, several European states have comprehensive policies regarding maternity, and even paternity, leaves. Little progress has been made on this front in the United States. In its report, *Listening to American Families,* the 1980 White House Conference on Families favored programs that would enable parents to hold jobs while minimizing disruption of family life.[11] But public support for such efforts has not been forthcoming, although some collective bargaining agreements carry maternity leave provisions and a substantial number of government workers are eligible for maternity leave.

FAMILIES AND THE LAW

Marriage and families always have had a special legal standing in our society. Normally the law has codified prevailing practices, but occasionally it has also reflected shifting social mores regarding families. Too frequently, however, law makers and judges have failed to anticipate the impact they will have.

Tax Law

The federal income tax codes are a prime example of how family impact was not fully considered in the legislative process. When the federal personal income tax was first levied in 1913, individuals were taxed on their own income regardless of marital status. An individual paid the same tax on adjusted gross income whether the person was married or single.

However, different property laws in the various states affected the individual's final tax liability. Some states had "community property" laws that stipulated that the income of a married couple belonged equally to both spouses. Married residents of these states reduced their total federal tax payments by claiming that each spouse was legally liable for the income tax due on 50 percent of the couple's total income, thereby escaping the rising progressive liability. In the rest of the states—the "common law" property states—the taxable income of an individual was unaffected by marital status. Suppose a couple is composed of a working husband who earns $15,000 a year and a wife who remains outside the labor force. In a "community property" state, the couple could have filed two individual returns for $7,500. However, in a "common law" property state, the working husband would have had to file a return covering the full $15,000. In 1920, the Supreme Court ruled (Poe v. Seaborn) that the residents in "community property" states could take advantage of this different tax treatment.

Eighteen years later, Congress reacted by allowing married couples to file joint returns. This gave all married couples some of the benefits of income splitting, but it also made tax obligations more dependent upon the type of household a person lived in. As the tax laws were amended further, the pendulum swung even more in the direction of factoring in family related variables into tax computations. Under current regulations, a married couple has the option of filing a joint return or two single returns—but there is a Catch 22 connected with the second option. If a married couple files two single returns, they cannot use the tax schedule for single individuals. Instead they must use a special tax rate schedule for married individuals filing separate returns, and the rates in this schedule raise the taxes due above the amount a single person with the same adjusted income would have to pay.

Prior to 1971 single persons were paying as much as 40 percent higher taxes compared to married couples with the same taxable income. While Congress felt that this entire differential should not be eliminated (i.e., tax obligations still should be affected by household status), the tax laws were amended so that a single person's taxes would be no more than about 20 percent above those of a married couple with the same income. Again, this change in the tax law, coupled with vast changes in the labor force participation patterns of women, had an impact that was not fully considered by Congress.

The changes have created a significant "marriage tax penalty," and a financial inducement to "living in sin." There even have been reports of couples who get divorced and then remarry to avoid paying taxes. The tax court proscribed such practices, but Uncle Sam's higher claims on the income of married couples persists. In 1979 the estimated added tax liability of 16 million couples exceeded $8 billion.[12]

The marriage tax penalty can be seen in the following example. Suppose a person earns $22,000 and has a spouse with no income. Using the standard deduction and filing jointly, this couple's 1980 tax bill would be roughly $3,200. Just by being married this wage earner will save $640, thanks to the nonworking spouse. The rules of the game change when both husband and wife report taxable income as a growing number of husbands and wives have been doing. The combined federal tax bill of a husband and wife each earning $22,000 apiece is about $11,100. However, if the same couple just shared quarters and eschewed marriage vows, the total tax obligation would be reduced by roughly $2,000. Also, as the earnings of the second wage earning spouse become a higher fraction of total family income, the nondivorce tax grows larger. For example, if the husband earns $20,000 and the wife earns $10,000, the couple will pay almost $600 more in taxes just because they are married. The size of the penalty, of course, increases as the husband's and wife's incomes rise, but it is still significant even for couples with very modest incomes. A couple earning $5,000 a year in 1980 could still save $150 in taxes by divorcing (figure 21).

Ideally the law might strive to achieve three basic household-related objectives: retain progressive rates; treat the family as a tax-paying unit; and establish "marriage neutrality." By being neutral toward marriage, the total tax bill would not be affected by household status. As Nancy Gordon has noted, any two of these goals can be obtained simultaneously, but all three cannot be achieved at the same time. The current system stresses the first two objectives at the expense of "neutrality."[13]

While a marriage tax penalty exists, its impact on actual marriage and family decisions is not at all clear. Nevertheless, some lawmakers proclaim that, by imposing "crushing taxation," the government is "doing all it can to destroy the family."[14] There are several policy responses that could eliminate the marriage tax penalty. One

FIGURE 21.

A tax penalty exists for married couples even with low family incomes.

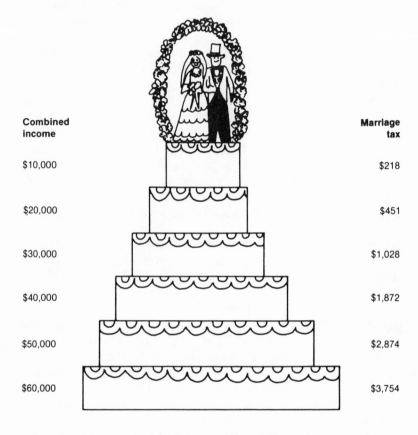

Combined income		Marriage tax
$10,000		$218
$20,000		$451
$30,000		$1,028
$40,000		$1,872
$50,000		$2,874
$60,000		$3,754

Source: U.S., Department of the Treasury, Office of Tax Analysis

way is to return to a system that requires mandatory individual filings. However, for more than one of five couples a system of mandatory individual filings would result in a significant boost in their tax obligations. A second policy response might be to maintain joint taxation on married couples but to let some portion of the second earner's income remain tax free. This would vastly reduce the marriage tax penalty. But assuming that the aggregate amount collected remains unchanged, it would increase the relative tax burden of single individuals and of families with only one wage earner, including single-parent families. Equity would dictate a reduction of tax burdens for these families rather than relative tax boosts.

For these reasons, the most workable and equitable policy would be to phase in optional individual filing. Under this proposal two-earner couples would have the option of filing either a joint return or separate individual returns. Many European countries have followed this option. There is a cost involved, however, in that optional individual filing would reduce revenues collected by the federal government. For this reason, it would be wise to phase in the optional system over a number of years. The "married filing separate returns" schedule could be adjusted over time so that it would more closely resemble the tax schedules for single individuals. President Carter favored this approach, and President Reagan proposed reducing the marriage tax.

Other government programs may also have an impact on marriage and fertility decisions. For example, social security regulations have made it profitable for some elderly couples not to marry because their benefits as a couple might be smaller than the total benefits they receive as single individuals. Also, several experiments with a negative income tax suggest that the added transfer income appears to have increased the chances that an individual in a bad marriage will seek a divorce. The negative income tax also can alter, in some cases, the fertility decisions of a family.[15]

Current tax laws make some provisions for the added costs of supporting children and other dependents. By granting exemptions and deductions for certain costs, the tax system recognizes that labor markets rarely consider family needs in establishing wage scales. The amount of the exemptions and deductions is not large enough to equal the added full costs of providing for these dependents, nor is it clear that they should. Only if a strong pro-natalist policy were warranted would a full cost subsidy be advisable. In effect, the current tax laws represent a compromise between a recognition that children represent an added financial burden for households and concerns that unchecked population growth is not what the United States requires. However, due to inflationary forces the size of these subsidies should be updated to reflect increasing costs of rearing children. Congress has increased these exemptions at infrequent intervals, and policymakers also have considered indexing these provisions so that regular periodic adjustments would keep pace with inflation. Yet indexing of these exemptions cannot be divorced from proposals to index the entire tax system, and it seems that this one exemption will not be tied to an automatic formula until Congress considers the entire tax system's relationship to indexing.

Other areas of the tax law also affect families. The tax system and social welfare efforts may induce the institutionalization of family members who could be taken care of in the home. For example, a larger portion of a medical bill may be paid by public programs if the ill person is placed in a hospital rather than treated at home. More liberal financial assistance for home treatment might send fewer people to hospitals and nursing homes if the family were able—and willing—to have these relatives remain at home. Tax credits can also better reflect the added burden caused by home treatment for family members with these difficulties. Not only are added costs involved, but some adults also may have to forego full-time employment because of a seriously ill child or relative. Public policy—both in the form of social services and the tax code—should be more sensitive to this situation. It is a sad commentary on our society if people are institutionalized only because the financial scales have been skewed in that direction—despite the wishes of a family and personal needs.

Family Disputes and the Law

The law is undergoing rapid transformations reflecting structural and economic family changes. Divorce, property settlements, and child custody proceedings have occupied a growing amount of judicial attention. Automobile accident cases still make up the majority of suits in court, but family-related cases are currently running a close second.

Also, a high incidence of violence within the family has come to light in recent years. Almost 1 million children may be neglected or abused each year, and as many as 2 million women may experience violence in the home.[16] What is not certain is whether the estimates of family violence represent a real upward trend or better data collection reflecting a heightened social concern for these issues. Having one separated or divorced parent kidnap a child from the other parent has become all too common an event.

The Office of Domestic Violence in the Department of Health and Human Services estimated that about one of four couples will undergo serious family violence during the course of a marriage or relationship. Roughly 25 percent of all homicides involve spouses, and 20 percent of all police deaths and 40 percent of police injuries occur when an officer responds to a "family violence" call.[17]

The old image of the presiding judge in juvenile and family courts, according to one legal scholar, was that of a wise and benevolent Solomon who could cut through all the legalisms and offer sage advice and counsel, as well as judgment. But times and mores have changed. The judge's maturity and wisdom is now most often expressed to a child's or family's lawyer, and the case had better not be handled in too informal a manner. At one time, family or juvenile courts may have been viewed as an implicit extension of social welfare agencies, but recently they have "rapidly become real courts of law."[18]

Family law has come a long way since Blackstone wrote on the subject two centuries ago. According to Blackstone, the legal existence of the woman was, in effect, suspended during marriage, or at least incorporated and consolidated into that of the husband. This meant that in case of a divorce, the father had the right to take custody of the children. All the wife's real and personal property was under the legal control of the husband. Under British common law, a husband had the right to beat his wife moderately as long as he used a stick no wider than his thumb.

State regulation of family relations clearly preceded the welfare society, but it remains a sensitive subject. For example, the Supreme Court held in 1878 that the state's power to regulate family structure superseded the Mormons' religious rights to practice polygamy. But states' rights to regulate family-related issues are constrained by practice and the equal protection and due process clauses of the Constitution. As one legal expert put it, "In family law, as perhaps nowhere else, the accumulated experience of our culture has a weight and standing of its own."[19] Rights of privacy and especially freedom from governmental intrusion into family affairs have been among our most important values. It is not true that regulation is growing in this area where freedom once flourished. In certain areas (e.g., sexual conduct) regulation has diminished. The recent trend has been to look at "compelling state interest" in judicial review of family laws. Few hard and fast rules have emerged, but in general, if courts have not found very compelling interests, they have struck down the regulations.

The courts are responding, however, albeit ever so slowly, to changing practice and life styles. For example, the "tender years" doctrine almost invariably resulted in a mother's being awarded the custody of her children. More recently, some courts apparently have considered that the fathers may be the better parents for the child, awarding them custody of their children. In what was reported to have been an unprecedented case, a Virginia circuit court awarded custody to an unwed father.[20] The Supreme Court has upheld zoning ordinances that forbid a commune from establishing itself in a residential area. But the high court has also acknowledged the right of females to abort pregnancies; possibly the most significant change in judicial actions affecting family structure.

With the family in a period of transition, the legal status of alimony is in a state of flux. States will be forced—more than ever before—to take a careful look at the rationality of family laws. Regulation of family affairs has always depended upon a difficult balancing between conflicting interests and values. There also has been a growing trend for federal courts to become involved in these issues. The Supreme Court in recent years has shown a far greater propensity than in the past to review family-related cases traditionally left to individual state courts.

INSTITUTIONAL LAGS

All too often the impact of institutions outside of the family have not been examined for their effects on households. Families do not exist in isolation from other social forces; labor markets, welfare legislation, tax regulations, and the legal system influence household structures.

While active family policies can have a positive impact on households, they are likely to respond very slowly to legislative mandates and institutional adjustments. Yet progress toward equality and equity can be steady, if deliberately pursued. There is no reason for following the course taken by Balzac's young hero and giving up on altering the social machinery as it affects families.

Part Four

THROUGH A MURKY LOOKING GLASS

Chapter Ten

THE QUEST FOR FULFILLMENT

A man's worst difficulties begin when he is able to do as he likes.

—Thomas Huxley

Freedom and discipline are indeed handmaidens; without the discipline of genuine love, freedom is invariably nonloving and destructive.

M. Scott Peck, *The Road Less Traveled*

EXPERIMENTATION

If Huxley's observation is correct, then the removal of many social constraints on individual behavior during recent years bodes lots of trouble for men and women. The legitimation of choice in household and sexual arrangements is far wider today than it ever was, even in the recent past. Subjective norms dominate sexual relations, replacing established societal rules and accepted constraints.

Beyond the data and statistical analysis, experimentation in household structures and love relationships have become major themes in modern literature. Science fiction writers have been among the vanguard in this effort, and Robert A. Heinlein's *Stranger in a Strange Land* is a prime example. Heinlein's hero, Michael Smith, is conceived by two earthlings during an interplanetary expedition to Mars. The entire crew perishes except, of course, Smith. In a new twist on an old plot, Mike is raised in Martian society and he returns to Earth when he is a young man.

Since Martian culture was well advanced and beyond the level of technology and ethics demonstrated by earthlings, Mike finds himself in the role of a prophet to a war-torn, restless, and unhappy Earth. The heart of the matter, Mike believes, is that human problems are caused by the way earthlings have handled sex and family relationships. Human sexual mores and family institutions have blocked a complete union, achieved by the Martians, and that accounts for earthly suffering.

The solution, according to Mike, is to form an environment in which men and women can realize their full potentials by "the joining of bodies with merging of souls in shared ecstasy, giving, receiving, delighting each other." Following Martian patterns, this includes establishing "nests," which are to replace conventional families. A nest is supposedly one big happy family in which sex is free among all members and in which jealousy is viewed as the ultimate vice. Similar to early Christian communities, a number of nests are formed as the good news spreads. But they are driven underground by the rest of society, and the young man from Mars is killed by a vengeful mob.

Not waiting for transportation to Mars, several groups have already tried to replicate Heinlein's nests on earth. The Kerista Movement, the Sexual Freedom League, and others have experimented with group marriages or extended "free" tribal family groups. Envisioned is a society holding certain property and assets in common, holding sexual partners in common, and providing for the communal raising of children. Utopian family forms have had a continuing appeal to fiction writers, science or conventional. Aldous Huxley, in *Island*, portrays a society composed of adoptive families that coexist with biological families in order to provide surrogate parents, alternative role models, and life experiences for children. His *Brave New World* did away with the family altogether. In B. F. Skinner's *Walden Two*, men and women are equal and entirely free. Poul Anderson's *Virgin Planet* shows a society in which serial marriage is the norm.

Old Wine?

The interest displayed by modern writers in exploring alternative or utopian family structures is in line with a long and honorable tradition. Titillating sex stories have commanded universal appeal from time immemorial, and the art of picturing ideal family structures that could enrich human relationships is a close runner-up, with a long-recorded history going all the way back to Plato. Sir Thomas More's *Utopia* contained such an alternative vision, and H. G. Wells's novel *Modern Utopia* shows how the subject continues to fascinate both writers and readers.

While past generations may have been thinkers, it could be argued that this generation is filled with doers. Instead of dreaming about achieving a blissful existence, people in this era are actively exploring what new forms and relationships can be created in reality. However, a closer examination indicates that the wisdom of Ecclesiastes holds true also in this era: "There is nothing new under the sun." Students of family history have noted how often modern utopian visions of the family are only old wine in new bottles. As Jessie Bernard has noted, the newer writers may fill their stories with computers and rocketships, but their underlying model of households and sexual relationships most often have been borrowed from writers of previous ages. These alternatives have been on the scene for a long time, and they are not peculiar to this age.

Still, applying the old adage that where there's smoke, there's fire, the constant battery of the family may lead to the conclusion that today's conditions are unique and that the family is on the verge of collapse. Again, such arguments can only be made if one loses all sense of historical perspective, as even a cursory review of nineteenth-century literature, when the bourgeois family was supposedly put on a pedestal, would amply demonstrate.[1]

Even when it comes to being doers and not just talkers, this age is not unique. The nineteenth-century was full of experimental communities that explored new family forms. John Humphrey Noyes's Oneida Community is illustrative and has been thoroughly recorded. The members of the community, which may have been the most successful and lasting, believed that Scripture should be taken quite literally when it commanded men and women to love one another. Sexual exclusiveness was done away with within the community. Not only was traditional marriage contrary to the Bible, Noyes and his followers believed, but it was also not in harmony with human nature.

Granted that alternative family structures have always existed, it has been argued that a growing number of individuals are availing themselves of these opportunities. Even this point is highly debatable. For example, while there has been a vast increase in the reported number of couples living together without the blessings of state or church, it is quite difficult to know how much of this shift is really a new trend. With diminished social pressures to follow any one pattern, a good portion of the reported increase in this behavior may represent only the increased willingness of people to be open about what has always taken place. "Swinging" is probably one of the oldest indoor sports known to humanity, as even a casual reader of the Bible would easily find, and not all of the participants were villains. What may be new is the willingness on the part of the players to publicly extol its virtues to the multitudes.

The evidence does not indicate that this era is buying into the utopian family visions at any greater rate than in the past. The subject stirs many fantasies, and it continues to fascinate, but it has not resulted in a significant number of people living under these arrangements. True, family life has changed in many ways in recent years, but it has not marched to the beat of any utopian drum. While data are difficult to obtain, it appears that relatively few Americans have experimented along the lines of Heinlein's nest or variations thereof. The presumed popularity of communes reflected more the interests of Sunday supplement writers in attracting readers than the actual numbers who participated in these living arrangements. More recently the headlines have been captured by homosexual marriages. Few group marriages (or other free extended families) remain viable for any considerable period of time. The longevity record of communal experiments appears to substantiate this.[2]

The current situation of these radical alternative family forms has much in common with the economist's notion of "effective demand." What keeps factories busy, workers employed, and taxes paid are not so much human desires, which may be insatiable, but the willingness and ability of consumers to purchase goods and services. Daydreaming and window shopping in front of a Rolls Royce dealer's showroom do not create jobs or enhance a country's gross national product. There appears to be quite a bit of daydreaming about alternatives to current family structures, but the effective demand remains very small.

The Israeli kibbutz is often pointed to as an example of an alternative form that has withstood the test of time. However, even in Israel the kibbutz model has attracted only a few people, remaining constant at about 3 percent of Israel's population. Also, the role of the nuclear family in the kibbutz has tended to expand in recent years. Kibbutz children are spending an increasingly significant amount of time with their parents, and many household tasks that were once the community's responsibility are now being returned to the family. For example, there has been a significant trend in having children sleep in their nuclear family's living quarters. Despite the vast interest in the kibbutz movement, being raised in this communal fashion is the exception rather than the rule in Israel.[3]

Subtle Changes

Whatever fantasies adult Americans may have about communal living, attitudinal research shows that only a small portion would opt for these alternative living styles. As indicated by the track record of many experiments, the reality rarely seems to provide as much pleasure as the dream. These fantasies may provide an escape valve, but the changes that have taken place in American families have been of a different sort than the ones pictured by most futurists. Even if alternatives to the nuclear family are not the wave of the future—or at least the near future—it does not mean that family life will not continue to evolve and change in many subtle ways. It does mean that there will be a continuum with the past instead of a radical break.

Current family forms are not the only, or probably not even the best, modes of living that the human mind and the economy could establish. History indicates that households have existed under numerous and different structures. In whatever direction the family is moving, the process of change is likely to be slow, as deeply embedded cultural values are not easily discarded. In most cases, divorced adults—even those who take off several years for experimentation—still return to more conventional family patterns, and cohabitation arrangements often have proven to be a way station en route to the altar or a transitional period rather than a permanent style of life.

Even proponents of "open marriages" have recognized this. A study sympathetic to the presumed new order found that some cohabitating couples followed "conventional" practices of allocating household work, while other couples who had a marriage license demonstrated more true sexual equality and freedom. They concluded that whether or not a marriage or relationship was "open" or "closed" depended on much more than its legal standing.[4]

The evidence does not indicate that departure from conventional family forms is any closer to fruition now than, say, in the 1950s. Just as increased trading of professional baseball players does not mean that the American public has given up on baseball, the presumably increased trading of partners does not mean a renouncement of marriage and families, but simply a change in the rules. The subtle changes that are occurring will affect the future of families far more than any unconventional arrangements or a few experimental communities.

MARXIST THEORY AND PRACTICE

The most sweeping, but short-lived, modern social experiment in family relations and marriage has taken place in the socialist countries. The results indicate that the family is much more than a bourgeois institution which is no longer required once the government has taken control of the means of production. The initial policy expressed by the Russian Bolsheviks was deeply hostile toward families and conventional marriage.

As a result of party policies, family bonds in the U.S.S.R. weakened, creating troublesome conflicts for the new rulers. Family disintegration was hindering other social goals such as rapid industrialization and the rearing and socialization of the next generation. As a result, the party line changed to incorporate stable family structure as an integral part of the progress toward socialism. Not only were the slogans changed, but Soviet family law shifted almost 180 degrees. There is a good deal to be learned about the need for families from the Soviet experiment and what happened to cause a change of heart within party circles.

Marxist Theory

Karl Marx and Friedrich Engels realized that their views on the family would evoke even more hostility than their calls to tear down capitalism. Yet they boldly called for the "abolition of the family," recognizing that this would be regarded as "the most . . . infamous proposal of the Communists." Denouncing "the bourgeois clap-trap about the family," they charged that "all family ties among the proletarians are torn asunder."[5]

Marx spent much time in a blistering analysis of existing family institutions rather than explain what household life would be like after the revolution. He argued that capitalist industrialization had destroyed—or corrupted—family bonds among workers. Long hours, child and female labor under poor working conditions and low wages, unemployment, alcoholism, and prostitution were all making a mockery of middle-class family mores. Even for the bourgeois, marriage was often reduced to nothing more than a legal arrangement to keep property and pass it down to the next generation.[6]

Engels continued to flesh out the Marxist theory of the family's role in the Communist scheme. Within the patriarchal family, he found "in miniature the same oppositions and contradictions as those in which society has been moving."[7] Under socialism the patriarchal family would be destroyed, and society would return to "pairing relationships." The interests of private property caused males to control females' sexual behavior, he insisted, in order to guarantee that their wealth would pass on to their offspring. However, marriages of convenience led to adultery and vice. He also predicted that the strongest upholders of the traditional patriarchal family would be the very same groups that had the largest vested interest in upholding the capitalist state.

Once private property was abolished, the need for the patriarchal family would be removed. Marriage, under most western laws, is more than a contract. Although marriage is entered into by a contract, it then becomes a legal status in the eyes of the state. In many other types of contracts, the parties can tear up the agreement without the approval of the state. However, even under modern no-fault divorce laws, the state must sanction a change in marriage status.[8] Under socialism, Engels asserted, it would be up to couples to decide how long they wanted to stay together, and they would not have to go to the state either to enter into or get out of a marriage. Early Communists saw (or conveniently misinterpreted) Engels's notions of "pairing relationships" as the equivalent of "free love."

Soviet Application

Within weeks of the revolution, Lenin signed a decree taking marriage and divorce completely out of the hands of the church. In line with the concept of pairing relationships, Lenin felt that the authority of the state should be limited to recording marriages, births, deaths, and divorces. Under the first Soviet family code, issued in 1918, even unregistered marriages had equal validity with registered marriages in the eyes of the law. In line with Engels's ideas, Lenin sensed that strong family ties could block the road toward developing a socialist state, and the role of families in the new Soviet society was downgraded. A divorce was easy and inexpensive to obtain. Even if only one party wanted the divorce, the marriage would be declared ended without a court hearing. In fact, at one point all that was required was for either the husband or wife to mail in a preprinted "divorce" postcard.

Under these regulations Soviet divorce rates climbed (although hard data are difficult to come by), and party officials became alarmed about the social instability that they believed was caused by family dissolution. Besides creating problems for raising the next generation, it was also felt that family instability had a negative spillover effect on productivity in the factories and farms. Starting in the 1930s, Soviet family policy took a dramatic shift. The state resumed the authority to pass regulations controlling the dissolution of marriage, just as in decadent capitalist nations, and unregistered marriages became illegal. With regard to child-support responsibilities, Soviet courts tended to be even stronger enforcers than their western counterparts. Significant declines in the fertility rate led Soviet officials to adopt policies that would ease the financial burden of having children. Stalin and the party press praised the virtues of a strong family as a basic building block in a healthy socialist state. As two American experts on Soviet family policy put it: "The wheel had turned full circle. The Soviet Union had been one of the easiest countries in the world in which to secure a divorce. Now it was one of the hardest. Getting a divorce in the U.S.S.R. today is rather like a tough obstacle race."[9]

Marxist social scientists have tried to explain the vast change in official attitudes toward the family as the logical development of a socialist society. When the Bolsheviks came to power in 1917, and when other communist parties took control of other eastern European nations following the Second World War, the family institutions were highly sexist, male dominated, and often used as a means of passing power and privilege down to the next generation. Also, some of the strongest advocates of the traditional family were religious and conservative opponents of the new system. In this context, the defense of the "family" often was a code word used to rally opposition to building a socialist society. Once the antisocialist forces were purged, the family could become a useful institution in obtaining the party's goals. At first the family was viewed, according to one Eastern European expert, as "the stronghold of private life and individualism, diverting attention and energy from public concerns and weakening the collective values." But as these "retrograde features" were removed, the family's "stability, its well-being, and the prevention of its malfunctioning or disruption were (seen as) extremely important."[10]

The neat picture provided by Marxist family analysts does not conform with—or explain—all the evidence or reasons for the shift in Soviet family policy. The birth rate—despite government efforts—remains quite low, and many Soviet couples have chosen to have only one child. Way before Western women's liberation movements encouraged women to enter the labor force, the typical Soviet wife and mother worked outside the household. But the bulk of low-paid Soviet workers are women, and sexual equality in the work force is still a distant goal. Even in the professions, female workers hold a significant chunk of the poorly paid teaching and medical jobs. For example, while women constitute 80 percent of the secondary classroom teachers, they account for only 27 percent of the heads of secondary schools. All predominantly female occupational groups in the U.S.S.R. have below-average incomes.[11]

Sexual equality within the Soviet household also has not been realized. The evidence indicates that the burden of shopping and housework falls disproportionately on working Soviet women. These responsibilities are more burdensome for Soviet women, as they regularly must stand in long queues to purchase consumer goods and do not enjoy advanced household technology to perform chores. As in the West, Soviet women often defer, and play a secondary role, to the men in their lives. The tradition of the extended family (three generations) is still a strong Russian institution. Even with the reputation of cradle-to-the-grave welfare, many Soviet families prefer to take care of their own younger and elderly members. Or as one Western observer noted: "Paradoxically at both ends of life—in childhood and old age—the system's deficiencies are strengthening the importance of the family."[12]

Russian family policies represent the most far-reaching modern efforts to redesign the role of the family. The Soviet experience supports the thesis that family stability is an essential ingredient for the achievement of social stability. Even in a vast welfare system, the family has been required to perform many functions that a collectivist state could not provide. It is an ironic twist that American conservatives and Soviet leaders are equally vociferous in advocating "pro-family" sentiments. In both cases the stability and authority of the family is seen as a necessary requirement to uphold and carry out radically different societal goals.

CONFLICTING ASPIRATIONS

Walter Lippmann noted that the "family is the inner citadel of religious authority and there the churches have taken their most determined stand." But in this area, as in others, the churches have lost their unquestioned authority. Religious leaders "have lost the exclusive right to preside over marriages. They have not been able to maintain the dogma that marriage is indissoluble," he noted.[13] Just as communist leaders have expressed fears that family dissolution could stand in the way of their goals, many Western religious and moral leaders have been very concerned that society could be debased by the shifts in family trends. As one theologian put it, American marriage mores have broken away from the biblical idea of "covenant" to one of just "contract." A contract can always be broken, but a covenant means that individuals exist under a higher order, which they are not free to dissolve. Others view divorce as a contagious disease. People now believe that it is all right to get a divorce if things are difficult, simply because so many other people are doing it.[14]

The Old Testament is tolerant of divorce and provides for the legal dissolution of marriage.[15] But Christ spoke out against this view. When asked by the Pharisees about divorce, Jesus responded: "What therefore God hath joined together, let not man put asunder. . . .Whosoever shall put away his wife, and marry another, committeth adultery against her. And if a woman shall put away her husband, and be married to another, she committeth adultery."[16]

The Roman Catholic Church has followed this injunction. However, some marriages may be annulled—for specific causes, such as nonconsummation or adultery. Religious authorities have always provided a safety valve—no matter how limited—to dissolve certain unions. However, the Catholic view is still that marriage "is effected by Divine power." Protestant theology tends to view marriage as a "holy estate," but one that can be terminated.[17]

Historical circumstances, in part, have led to the Protestant views concerning divorce. The immediate cause for the founding of the Church of England was in large measure a royal divorce. However, during the seventeenth and eighteenth centuries, legal divorce and remarriage in England was only for the very rich—and by folk customs for the very poor. For the vast majority it was impossible because of the great costs involved or the dire social stigma associated with ending a marriage. With the rise of political and economic liberalism and notions of individual liberty, civil authorities in many of the Protestant countries established divorce acts that expanded the grounds on which a marriage could be ended. Protestant theologians often found themselves in the position of conceding to the new powers of the civil authorities, and biblical justifications were found for shifting views on divorce.[18]

Other religions have recognized the right of divorce. Muhammad countenanced divorce only as a last resort, and he stated that nothing displeased God more than the disruption of marital vows, but the Koran makes provision for divorce. The traditional Jewish marriage contract contains clauses providing the wife with certain financial means and assets if the marriage is ended.

New Freedom?

With a diminution of the hold of religious authority, new freedoms—if not new disciplines—have emerged as religious and social regulations and controls over marital behavior have declined. While a calculus for measuring happiness is yet to be designed, some evidence indicates that the new-found freedoms have not always led to an increased sense of serenity for many individuals. A growing number of individuals experiencing family dissolution find that they have rejected old codes of behavior without devising new controls to fill the vacuum. Or as one researcher of shifting sexual and family mores put it: "The freedom to cross the frontiers is of no value to people immobilized by anxiety and inadequacy."[19]

The rejection of old codes raises the question whether the traditional family model remains suitable for a modern free democratic society that places pluralism and individualism on a pedestal. However, unlike totalitarian or theocratic societies that have one official ideology—or state religion—backing up the system, the price of new sexual and household freedoms in free societies may be a sense of drift or emptiness. It will often appear that we are at a loss as one structure is torn down and no new firm edifice is seen going up in its place. A growing number of Americans seem to be facing a conflict between establishing a stable family structure (including the rearing of children) and the desire to achieve immediate, satisfying relationships.

Predictions of the future are always fraught with difficulties, yet turning the clock back to an older family system does not appear to be in the offing. In the near future, the divorce rate will remain high, and the number of children living with both natural parents may continue to decline. Family breakup may not be growing at as high a rate as in the recent past, but it would be unrealistic to expect it to fall back to the levels of a generation ago. Also, it is reasonable to anticipate that fertility rates of women in the 1980s will not come close to the levels attained by their mothers. The single-parent family is likely to remain a feature on the American scene for the balance of the twentieth century, and this will require government efforts to counter the economic and social inequalities experienced by individuals in this type of household structure.

Women—many of them wives and mothers—will continue to make a significant impact in the labor force. Sexual discrimination on the job and in household chores will be slow in changing, but the long-run trend should be toward greater equality on both fronts.

In essence, there will be no one dominant family type or structure. The husband-wife-children household will not represent the majority of families. Instead living arrangements will demonstrate a higher degree of pluralism, and it will require a greater degree of flexibility in public policies to cope with the diverse needs of different household types.

The United States is not alone in undergoing these family changes; other industrialized nations have experienced a similar pattern. The expansion of the welfare state has been more a reaction to these developments than their prime cause. A compassionate and affluent society that moves beyond the bounds of strict laissez-faire should make it a priority to assure that children are not denied basic goods and services because of their household structure. This could prove to be one of the richest investments society could make.

New Discontents?

Freud noted the inevitable antagonism between an individual's aspirations or instincts and the strictures civilization places on the individual. He concluded that civilization is made possible only by individual renouncement, and that a sense of guilt shapes civilized society. While society provides many benefits for the individual, it also produces a series of discontents. A similar process characterizes family life. Families are made possible by the repression of certain actions and desires.

The current discontent concerning families is caused not only by a conflict between striving for social stability versus individual freedom, but also by the uncertainty of its future structure. The older pattern may have been dominated by sexism and lives of quiet desperation, but it did provide society and individuals with a sense of security. The new patterns of sexual behavior and living arrangements are bound to produce their own anxieties. To some it may ppear that families are falling apart with nothing to take their place. The scars of a broken home may be difficult to heal, but the pressures within many traditional families are also strong enough to create neurotic personalities. However, despite these discontents, the institution appears to have more strength and resilience than it is often accredited with.

Joseph Fletcher, the Episcopalian theologian, noted that "free love is an ideal. Unfortunately, it is an ideal of which very few of us are capable."[20] Yet the important question seems to be: Is the ideal of real equality between husband and wife possible in a growing number of homes? This problem is not just a matter of concern to Western societies. Marxist nations, including the Soviet Union and China, demonstrate that sexual inequality in the home and on the job is pervasive and not just a feature of capitalism. Can men and women share power, responsibilities, and opportunities in a far greater way than in the past? If the answer is affirmative, then the families that will emerge from this wrenching period will tend to be based on stronger foundations than in previous eras. Ibsen's Nora will not have to leave home—or her dollhouse—and turn her back on marriage. Instead she, and the many millions who followed her, will be able to find self-actualization or wholeness within the family.

The crux of the matter is that there will be no simple or easy solution to these often seemingly irremediable conflicts. Judging from its final report, *Listening to America's Families*, this situation was painfully rediscovered by the White House Conference on Families. Yet most families will continue to do what they have always done—cope as best they can in the face of shifting obstacles. Freud was correct in referring to families as the "germ cells" of civilization. The direction of the type of society and economy we envisage, and, in fact, create, will depend in large measure on how this basic institution functions and evolves. Currently fashionable gloom and doom scenarios miss the essential process of adjustment and change. Meeting these challenges, and not singing funeral dirges for the family, will provide our greatest opportunities and our greatest hope.

NOTES

CHAPTER ONE

1. M. Rostovtzeff, *A History of the Ancient World*, 2 vols. (Oxford: Clarendon Press, 1927), 2: 364.

2. Robert L. Heilbroner, *An Inquiry into the Human Prospect* (New York: W. W. Norton and Co., 1974), p. 15.

3. Bertrand Russell, *Marriage and Morals* (New York: Horace Liveright Co., 1929), p. 173.

4. Pat Mainardi, "The Politics of Housework," in *Sisterhood Is Powerful*, ed. Robin Morgan (New York: Vintage Books, 1970), p. 448.

5. François Raveau, "Future Family Patterns and Society," in *The Family and Its Future*, ed. Katherine Elliott (London: J. & A. Churchill, 1970), pp. 43–44.

6. Gary S. Becker, "A Theory of Marriage," in *Economics of the Family: Marriage, Children, and Human Capital*, ed. Theodore W. Schultz (Chicago: University of Chicago Press, 1973), p. 299.

7. Margaret Mead, "The Impact of Cultural Changes on the Family," in *The Family in the Urban Community* (Detroit: Merrill-Palmer School, 1953), p. 4.

8. Victor R. Fuchs, *The Service Economy* (New York: Columbia University Press, 1968), p. 11.

9. U.S., Department of Health, Education, and Welfare, "Formulating National Policies on Child and Family Development" (1978, processed), p. 7.

10. George Gallup, *American Families—1980* (Princeton, N.J.: Gallup Organization, 1980), pp. 1, 23.

11. Paul C. Glick and Arthur J. Norton, "Marrying, Divorcing, and Living Together in the U.S. Today," *Population Bulletin* 32, no. 5 (1979): 36–37.

12. U.S., Department of Commerce, Bureau of the Census, *Divorce, Child Custody, and Child Support* (Washington, D.C.: Government Printing Office, 1979), series P–23, no. 84, p. 3.

13. Richard E. Leakey and Roger Lewin, *People of the Lake: Mankind and Its Beginnings* (Garden City, N.Y.: Doubleday & Co., 1978), p. 121.

14. Dena Kleiman, "Many Young Women Now Say They'd Pick Family over Career," *New York Times*, 28 December 1980, pp. 1, 28.

CHAPTER TWO

1. U.S., Congress, House Committee on Education and Labor, *Hearings on the White House Conference on Families* (Washington, D.C.: Government Printing Office, 1978), pp. 481–83.

2. Louis Harris and Associates, *The Playboy Report on American Men* (Chicago: Playboy Press, 1979), pp. 9–11; and George Gallup, *American Families—1980* (Princeton, N.J.: Gallup Organization, 1980), p. 29.

3. *Public Opinion* (June/July 1979), p. 34.

4. Stephen Rawlings, *Perspectives on American Husbands and Wives* (Washington, D.C.: Government Printing Office, 1978), series P–23, no. 77, pp. 3–4.

5. U.S., Department of Commerce, Bureau of the Census, *Historical Statistics of the United States—Colonial Times to 1957* (Washington, D.C.: Government Printing Office, 1957), pp. A-210–14.

6. Philip J. Greven, Jr., *Four Generations: Population, Land, and Family in Colonial Andover, Massachusetts* (Ithaca, N.Y.: Cornell University Press, 1970), p. 121.

7. Paul C. Glick and Arthur J. Norton, "Marrying, Divorcing, and Living Together in the U.S. Today," *Population Bulletin* 32, no. 5 (1979): 6.

8. Ira L. Reiss, *Family Systems in America* (Hinsdale, Ill.: Dryden Press, 1976), pp. 173–81.

9. Gerald R. Leslie, *The Family in Social Context* (New York: Oxford University Press, 1976), pp. 688–91.

10. Gary S. Becker, "A Theory of Marriage," in *Economics of the Family: Marriage, Children, and Human Capital*, ed. Theodore W. Schultz (Chicago: University of Chicago Press, 1973), pp. 301–4.

11. Jessie Bernard, *The Future of Marriage* (New York: Bantam Books, 1973), p. 17.

12. Ibid., p. 19.

13. U.S., Department of Commerce, Bureau of the Census, *Divorce, Child Custody, and Child Support* (Washington, D.C.: Government Printing Office, 1979), series P–23, no. 84, pp. 1, 7.

14. U.S., Department of Commerce, Bureau of the Census, *Marital Status and Living Arrangements: March 1978* (Washington, D.C.: Government Printing Office, 1979), series P–20, no. 338, pp. 3, 12.

15. Mary Jo Bane, *Here to Stay: American Families in the Twentieth Century* (New York: Basic Books, 1976), p. 30, appendix A–6.

16. James A. Weed, "Age at Marriage as a Factor in State Divorce Rate Differentials," *Demography* (August 1974), p. 361.

17. Phillip Cutright, "Income and Family Events: Marital Stability," *Journal of Marriage and the Family* (May 1971), pp. 304–6.

18. Andrew James Cherlin, *Social and Economic Determinants of Marital Separation* (Employment and Training Administration, U.S., Department of Labor, 1976, processed), pp. 50–52.

19. M. F. Nimkoff, *The Family* (Boston: Houghton-Mifflin, 1934), p. 446.

20. Bane, *Here to Stay*, pp. 32–33.

21. Heather L. Ross and Isabel V. Sawhill, *Time of Transition: The Growth of Families Headed by Women* (Washington, D.C.: Urban Institute, 1975), pp. 19–21.

CHAPTER THREE

1. *Wall Street Journal*, 15 October 1979, p. 24.

2. Ansley Coale and Melvin Zelnick, *New Estimates of Fertility and Population in the United States* (Princeton, N.J.: Princeton University Press, 1963), p. 36.

3. Richard A. Easterlin, "The American Population," in *American Economic Growth: An Economist's History of the United States*, ed. Lance E. Davis et al. (New York: Harper & Row, 1972), pp. 123–27.

4. U.S., Department of Commerce, Bureau of the Census, *Fertility of American Women: June 1978* (Washington, D.C.: Government Printing Office, 1979), Current Population Reports, series P–20, no. 341, pp. 5, 66.

5. U.S., Department of Commerce, Bureau of the Census, *Estimates of the Population of the United States and the Components of Change: 1940 to 1978* (Washington, D.C.: Government Printing Office, 1979), series P–25, no. 802, pp. 2, 8.

6. Charles F. Westoff, "Marriage and Fertility in the Developed Countries," *Scientific American* (December 1978), p. 51.

7. Maurice J. Moore and Martin O'Connell, *Perspectives on American Fertility* (Washington, D.C.: Government Printing Office, 1978), series P–23, no. 70, p. 9.

8. Thomas Malthus, *Population: The First Essay* (Ann Arbor, Mich.: University of Michigan Press, 1959), p. 5.

9. Richard A. Easterlin, Michael L. Wachter, and Susan M. Wachter, "Here Comes Another Baby Boom," *Wharton Magazine* (Summer 1979), pp. 29–30.

10. U.S., Department of Labor, Women's Bureau, *The Earnings Gap Between Women and Men* (Washington, D.C., Government Printing Office, 1979), p. 2; and U.S., Department of Commerce, Bureau of the Census, *Money Income of Families and Persons in the United States: 1979* (Washington, D.C.: Government Printing Office, 1980), series P–60, no. 125, p. 23.

11. William P. Butz and Michael P. Ward, *Countercyclical U.S. Fertility and Its Implications* (Santa Monica, Calif.: Rand Corporation, 1978), pp. 9–10.

12. U.S., Department of Commerce, Bureau of the Census, *Characteristics of American Children and Youth* (Washington, D.C.: Government Printing Office, 1978), series P–23, no. 66, p. 31.

13. *Public Opinion* (October/November 1979), p. 17.

14. Kristin A. Moore and Sandra L. Hofferth, "Women and Their Children," in *The Subtle Revolution: Women at Work*, ed. Ralph E. Smith (Washington, D.C.: Urban Institute, 1979), pp. 128–32.

15. Robert Weller, "Wives' Employment and Cumulative Family Size in the United States," *Demography* (February 1977), pp. 47–49.

16. James Cramer, "Births, Expected Family Size and Poverty," in *Five Thousand American Families: Patterns of Economic Progress*, 5 vols., ed. James N. Morgan et al. (Ann Arbor, Mich.: Survey Research Center of the University of Michigan, 1974–77), 2: 279.

17. Greg J. Duncan, "Educational Attainment," in Morgan, *Five Thousand American Families*, 1: 317–20.

18. Peter H. Lindert, "Sibling Position and Achievement," *Journal of Human Resources* (Spring 1977), p. 209.

19. Russell Hill and Frank Stafford, "Time Inputs to Children," in Morgan, *Five Thousand American Families*, 2: 333–36.

20. Russell Hill and Frank Stafford, "Allocation of Time to Preschool Children and Educational Opportunity," *Journal of Human Resources* (Summer 1974), p. 339.

21. Greg J. Duncan, "Paths to Economic Well-Being," in Morgan, *Five Thousand American Families*, 5: 193.

22. Paul C. Glick and Arthur J. Norton, "Marrying, Divorcing, and Living Together in the U.S. Today," *Population Bulletin* 32, no. 5 (1979): 20–21.

CHAPTER FOUR

1. *Public Opinion* (December/January 1980), pp. 22–23.

2. U.S., Department of Health, Education, and Welfare, National Center for Health Statistics, *Final Divorce Statistics* 28, no. 2 (Washington, D.C.: Government Printing Office, 1979), p. 4.

3. U.S., Department of Commerce, Bureau of the Census, *Marital Status and Living Arrangements* (Washington, D.C.: Government Printing Office, 1979), series P–20, no. 338, p. 27; and Paul C. Glick and Arthur J. Norton, "Marrying, Divorcing, and Living Together in the U.S. Today," *Population Bulletin* 32, no. 5 (1979): 28.

4. U.S., Department of Commerce, Bureau of the Census, *Marriage, Divorce, Widowhood, and Remarriage by Family Characteristics* (Washington, D.C.: Government Printing Office, 1977), series P–20, no. 312, p. 16.

5. U.S., Department of Commerce, Bureau of the Census, *Marital Status and Living Arrangements* (Washington, D.C.: Government Printing Office, 1979), series P–20, no. 338, p. 28.

6. Mary Jo Bane, *Here to Stay: American Families in the Twentieth Century* (New York: Basic Books, 1976), pp. 12–13.

7. Melvin Zelnik and John F. Kanter, "Unprotected Intercourse Among Unwed Teenagers," *Family Planning Perspective* (January/February 1975), p. 39; idem, "Sexual Activity, Contraceptive Use and Pregnancy Among Metropolitan Area Teenagers: 1971–1979," *Family Planning Perspective* (September/October 1980), p. 234.

8. Audrey E. Jones and Paul J. Placek, "Teenage Women in the U.S.A.: Sex, Contraception, Pregnancy, Fertility, and Maternal and Infant Health," in *Teenage Pregnancy and Family Impact: New Perspectives on Policy*, ed. Theodora Ooms et al. (Washington, D.C.: Family Impact Seminar of the George Washington University, 1979), p. 14.

9. Frank Furstenberg, Jr., "Burdens and Benefits: The Impact of Early Childbearing on the Family," in Ooms, *Teenage Pregnancy and Family Impact*, p. 21.

10. Kristin A. Moore et al., *Teenage Motherhood: Social and Economic Consequences* (Washington, D.C.: Urban Institute, 1979), pp. 9, 38, 43.

11. Arthur Campbell, "The Role of Family Planning in the Reduction of Poverty," *Journal of Marriage and the Family* (May 1968), p. 236.

12. Maurice J. Moore and Martin O'Connell, *Perspective on American Fertility* (Washington, D.C.: Government Printing Office, 1978), series P–23, no. 70, p. 46.

13. Richard Lingeman, *Small Town America* (New York: Putnam, 1980) as cited by Walter Clemons, "Of Sleepers and Swings," *Newsweek* 28 July 1980, p. 65.

14. Willard Waller, *The Old Love and the New* (New York: Liveright & Co., 1930), pp. 22–23.

15. William J. Goode, *Women in Divorce* (New York: Free Press, 1965), pp. 317–18.

16. Sheldon Glueck and Eleanor Glueck, *Unraveling Juvenile Delinquency* (Cambridge, Mass.: Harvard University Press, 1950), p. 91; idem, *Delinquents and Nondelinquents in Perspective* (Cambridge, Mass.: Harvard University Press, 1968), p. 88.

17. Charles J. Browning, "Differential Impact of Family Disorganization Upon Male Adolescents," *Social Problems* (Summer 1960), p. 43.

18. Lee Burchinal, "Characteristics of Adolescents from Unbroken, Broken and Reconstituted Families," *Journal of Marriage and the Family* (February 1964), pp. 48–50.

19. F. Ivan Nye, "Child Adjustment in Broken and Unhappy Unbroken Homes," *Marriage and Family Living* (November 1957), pp. 360–61.

20. Judson T. Landis, "The Trauma of Children When Parents Divorce," *Marriage and Family Living* (February 1960), pp. 10–11.

21. Judson T. Landis, "Social Correlates of Divorce and Nondivorce Among the Unhappy Married," *Marriage and Family Living* (May 1963), p. 179; Benjamin Schlesinger and Eugene Stasiuk, "Children of Divorced Parents in Second Marriages," in *Children of Separation and Divorce*, ed. Irving R. Stuart and Lawrence Edwin (New York: Grossman, 1972), pp. 21–22.

22. Joan B. Kelly and Judith S. Wallerstein, "Children of Divorce," *Principal* (October 1979), p. 55.

23. William G. Bowen and T. Aldrich Finegan, *The Economics of Labor Force Participation* (Princeton, N.J.: Princeton University Press, 1969), pp. 397, 411.

24. Albert Rees and Wayne Gray, *Family Effects in Youth Employment*, National Bureau of Economic Research (Cambridge, Mass., 1979, processed), p. 8.

25. Alvin L. Schorr, *Public Policies and Single Parents* (1979 processed), p. 12.

26. National Commission for Employment Policy, *Report on Single Heads of Households* (1979, processed), p. 6.

27. U.S., Department of Commerce, Bureau of the Census, *Child Support and Alimony: 1978* (Washington, D.C.: Government Printing Office, 1980), series P–23, pp. 6–7 (advance report).

28. Nancy M. Gordon, Carol A. Jones, and Isabel V. Sawhill, *The Determinants of Child Support Payments* (Washington, D.C.: Urban Institute, 1978), pp. 17, 18, 20.

29. Carol A. Jones, Nancy M. Gordon, and Isabel V. Sawhill, *Child Support Payments in the United States* (Washington, D.C.: Urban Institute, 1976), p. 14.

30. Greg J. Duncan and James N. Morgan, "An Overview of Part 1 Findings," in *Five Thousand American Families: Patterns of Economic Progress*, 5 vols., ed. James N. Morgan et al. (Ann Arbor, Mich.: Survey Research Center of the University of Michigan, 1974–77), 5: 11.

CHAPTER FIVE

1. *New York Times*, 12 September 1976, p. 1.

2. *Public Opinion* (December/January 1980), pp. 24–25.

3. Judith Ann, "The Secretarial Proletariat," in *Sisterhood Is Powerful*, ed. Robin Morgan (New York: Vintage Books, 1970), p. 100.

4. Eleanor Flexner, *Century of Struggle: The Women's Rights Movement in the United States* (New York: Atheneum Publishers, 1968), p. 9.

5. Don D. Lescohier, "Working Conditions," in *History of Labor in the United States*, 4 vols., ed. John R. Commons et al. (New York: Macmillan Co., 1935),3: 36–37.

6. Cited in Elizabeth Faulkner Baker, *Technology and Women's Work* (New York: Columbia University Press, 1964), p. 6.

7. William H. Chafe, "Looking Backward in Order to Look Forward: Women, Work, and Social Values in America," in *Women and the American Economy: A*

Look to the 1980s, ed. Juanita M. Kreps (Englewood Cliffs, N.J.: Prentice-Hall, 1976), pp. 6–7.

8. Francine D. Blau, "The Data on Women Workers: Past, Present, and Future," in *Women Working: Theories and Facts in Perspective*, ed. Ann H. Stromberg et al. (Palo Alto, Calif.: Mayfield Publishing Co., 1978), p. 33.

9. "Prefatory Letter from Theodore Roosevelt," in Mrs. John Van Vorst and Marie Van Vorst, *The Woman Who Toils* (New York: Doubleday, Page, & Co., 1903), p. 2.

10. Walter Houghton, *The Victorian Frame of Mind* (New Haven, Conn.: Yale University Press, 1957), p. 343.

11. Christopher Lasch, *Haven in a Heartless World: The Family Besieged* (New York: Basic Books, 1977), pp. 5–6.

12. U.S., Department of Commerce, Bureau of the Census, *Historical Statistics of the United States: Colonial Times to 1957* (Washington, D.C.: Government Printing Office, 1960), p. 72.

13. Blau, "Data on Women Workers," in Stromberg et al., *Women Working*.

14. The National Commission on Employment and Unemployment Statistics, *Counting the Labor Force* (Washington, D.C.: Government Printing Office, 1979), p. 43.

15. Elizabeth Brandeis, "Labor Legislation," in Commons et al., *History of Labor*, 3: 511–12.

16. Tony Tanner, *Adultery in the Novel: Contract and Transgression* (Baltimore, Md.: Johns Hopkins University Press, 1979), p. 373.

17. William G. Bowen and T. Aldrich Finegan, *The Economics of Labor Force Participation* (Princeton, N.J.: Princeton University Press, 1969), p. 28.

18. Jacob Mincer and Solomon Polachek, "Family Investments in Human Capital: Earnings of Women," in *Economics of the Family: Marriage, Children, and Human Capital*, ed. Theodore W. Schultz (Chicago: University of Chicago Press, 1973), p. 397.

19. Allyson Sherman Grossman, "Children of Working Mothers," *Monthly Labor Review* (January 1978), p. 31.

20. Carol Ireson, "Girls' Socialization for Work," in Stromberg et al., *Women Working*, pp. 181–82, 186.

21. Barbara R. Bergmann, "Reducing the Pervasiveness of Discrimination," in *Jobs for Americans*, ed. Eli Ginzberg (Englewood Cliffs, N.J.: Prentice-Hall, 1976), pp. 134–35.

22. U.S., Department of Commerce, Bureau of the Census, *Money Income and Poverty Status of Families and Persons in the United States: 1978* (Washington, D.C.: Government Printing Office, 1979), pp. 18–19; idem, *Employment and Earnings* (January 1979), p. 184.

23. *Employment and Training Report of the President* (Washington, D.C.: Government Printing Office, 1979), p. 107.

24. Francine D. Blau and Wallace E. Hendricks, "Occupational Segregation by Sex: Trends and Prospects," *Journal of Human Resources* (Spring 1979), pp. 208–9.

25. Stephen Rawlings, *Perspectives on American Husbands and Wives* (Washington, D.C.: Government Printing Office, 1978), series P–23, no. 77, p. 33.

26. Isabel V. Sawhill et al., *Income Transfers and Family Structure* (Washington, D.C.: Urban Institute, 1975), p. 3.

27. F. Ivan Nye, "Husband-Wife Relationship," in *Working Mothers*, ed. Lois Wladis Hoffman and F. Ivan Nye (San Francisco: Jossey-Bass, 1974), pp. 205–6.

28. Sandra L. Hofferth and Kristin A. Moore, "Women's Employment and Marriage," in *The Subtle Revolution: Women at Work*, ed. Ralph E. Smith (Washington,

D.C.: Urban Institute, 1979), pp. 113–15; Frank P. Stafford. "Women's Use of Time Converging with Men's." *Monthly Labor Review* (December 1980), pp. 57–58.

29. Maximiliane E. Szinovacz, "Role Allocation, Family Structure, and Female Employment," *Journal of Marriage and the Family* (November 1977), p. 790.

30. U.S., Congressional Budget Office, *Child Care and Preschool: Options for Federal Support* (Washington, D.C.: Government Printing Office, 1978), p. 12; and Mary Jo Bane et al., "Child Care Settings in the United States," in *Child Care and Mediating Structures*, ed. Brigitte Berger and Sidney Callahan (Washington, D.C.: American Enterprise Institute, 1979), p. 19.

31. "OEO Child Care Program; Veto Sustained in the Senate," *Congressional Quarterly Almanac* (Washington: Congressional Quarterly, 1971), p. 504.

32. Mary Jo Bane, *Here to Stay: American Families in the Twentieth Century* (New York: Basic Books, 1976), p. 17.

33. Thomas M. Stanback, Jr., *Understanding the Service Economy: Employment, Productivity, Location* (Baltimore, Md.: Johns Hopkins University Press, 1979), p. 49.

CHAPTER SIX

1. Arthur W. Calhoun, *A Social History of the American Family: From Colonial Times to the Present*, 3 vols. (New York: Barnes & Noble, 1945), 3: 184.

2. U.S., Department of Labor, Office of Policy Planning and Research, *The Negro Family: The Case for National Action* (Washington, D.C.: Government Printing Office, 1965), pp. 5, 29, 35, 39, 47.

3. William Ryan, "Savage Discovery—The Moynihan Report," in *The Black Family: Essays and Studies*, ed. Robert Staples (Belmont, Calif: Wadsworth Publishing Co., 1971), p. 58.

4. Robert B. Hill, *The Strengths of Black Families* (New York: National Urban League, 1971), pp. 6, 9, 31.

5. Christopher Lasch, *Haven in a Heartless World: The Family Besieged* (New York: Basic Books, 1977), pp. 159–60.

6. Sar A. Levitan, *The Great Society's Poor Law: A New Approach to Poverty* (Baltimore, Md.: Johns Hopkins Press, 1969), p. 282.

7. Ira L. Reiss, *Family Systems in America* (Hinsdale, Ill.: Dryden Press, 1976), p. 363.

8. Tom Wolfe, *Mauve Gloves and Madmen, Clutter and Vine* (New York: Bantam Books, 1977), p. 188; Eldridge Cleaver, *Soul on Ice* (New York: McGraw-Hill, 1968), p. 152.

9. Betty Friedan, "Feminism Takes a New Turn," *New York Times Magazine*, 8 November 1979, pp. 40, 92.

10. Frank L. Mott, *The Socioeconomic Status of Households Headed by Women* (Washington, D.C.: Government Printing Office, 1979), pp. 10, 29, 45, 52.

11. Frank L. Mott and Sylvia F. Moore, "The Causes and Consequences of Marital Breakdown," in *Women, Work, and Family*, ed. Frank L. Mott (Lexington, Mass.: Lexington Books, 1978), pp. 123–24.

12. Liz B. Shaw, *Economic Consequences of Marital Disruption* (Columbus, Ohio: Center for Human Resource Research of the Ohio State University, 1978), pp. 16, 19.

13. Gerald R. Leslie, *The Family in Social Context* (New York: Oxford University Press, 1976), pp. 300–301.

14. Elaine Morgan, *The Descent of Woman* (New York: Stein and Day, 1972), pp. 243–44.

15. Heather L. Ross and Isabel V. Sawhill, *Time of Transition: The Growth of Families Headed by Women* (Washington, D.C.: Urban Institute, 1975), pp. 25, 30, 160.

16. Lasch, *Haven in a Heartless World*, p. 162.

17. Simone de Beauvoir, *The Second Sex* (New York: Bantam Books, 1961), p. 654.

18. Germaine Greer, *The Female Eunuch* (New York: McGraw-Hill, 1971), p. 233.

CHAPTER SEVEN

1. Robert L. Heilbroner, *The Economic Problem* (New York: Prentice-Hall, 1972),p. 89.

2. Jean Y. Jones, *The American Family: Problems and Federal Policies* (Washington, D.C.: Congressional Research Service, 1977), pp. 2–3.

3. William J. Goode, *The Family* (New York: Prentice-Hall, 1964), p. 108.

4. Nancy S. Barrett, "The Politics of Family Policy" (Washington, D.C.: Urban Institute, 1979, processed), p. 4.

5. Jimmy Carter, "The American Family: A Campaign Statement in Manchester, N.H." (processed), 3 August 1976.

6. Christopher Lasch, *Haven in a Heartless World: The Family Besieged* (New York: Basic Books, 1977), p. 100.

7. Jacques Donzelot, *The Policing of Families* (New York: Pantheon Books, 1979), pp. 94–95.

8. *Public Opinion* (December/January 1980), pp. 20–21.

9. Martin Rein, *Notes for the Study of Tacit Family Policy* (Cambridge, Mass.: Joint Center for Urban Studies of M.I.T. and Harvard University, 1977), p. 2.

10. George Masnick and Mary Jo Bane, *The Nation's Families: 1960–1990* (Cambridge, Mass.: Joint Center for Urban Studies of M.I.T. and Harvard University, 1980), p. 57.

11. Carol Glassman, "Women and the Welfare System," in *Sisterhood Is Powerful,* ed. Robin Morgan (New York: Vintage Books, 1970), p. 102.

12. White House Conference on Families, *Listening to America's Families* (Washington, D.C.: Government Printing Office, 1980).

13. Gunnar Myrdal, *Population: A Problem for Democracy* (Cambridge, Mass.: Harvard University Press, 1940), p. 74.

14. Alva Myrdal, *Nation and Family: The Swedish Experiment in Democratic Family and Population Policy* (Cambridge, Mass.: M.I.T. Press, 1941),p. 27.

15. Jarl Lindgren, "Finland," in *Family Policy: Government and Families in Fourteen Countries,* ed. Sheila B. Kamerman and Alfred J. Kahn (New York: Columbia University Press, 1978), p. 270.

16. Gunnar Myrdal, *Beyond the Welfare State* (London: Methuen & Co., 1960), p. 24.

17. Rita Liljestrom, "Sweden," in Kamerman and Kahn, eds., *Family Policy,* pp. 25–26.

18. Sheila B. Kamerman and Alfred J. Kahn, "Europe's Innovative Family Policies," *Trans-Atlantic Perspective* (March 1980), p. 10.

19. The Family Impact Seminar of George Washington University, "Recommendations to the White House Conference on Families" (processed, 1980), p. 4.

20. Bruno Stein, *Social Security and Pensions in Transition* (New York: Free Press, 1980), pp. 15, 35.

21. U.S., Department of Commerce, Bureau of the Census, *Money Income and Poverty Status of Families and Persons in the United States: 1978* (Washington, D.C.: Government Printing Office, 1979), series P–60, no. 120, pp. 24–25.

22. Harold W. Watts and Felicity Skidmore, *The Implications of Changing Family Patterns and Behavior for Labor Force and Hardship Measurement* (Washington: National Commission on Employment and Unemployment Statistics, 1978), p. 9.

23. U.S., Congressional Budget Office, *Poverty Status of Families Under Alternative Definitions of Income* (Washington, D.C.: Government Printing Office, 1977), paper no. 17, p. 29.

24. Robert D. Plotnick and Felicity Skidmore, *Progress against Poverty* (New York: Academic Press, 1975), p. 147.

CHAPTER EIGHT

1. Nancy M. Gordon, "Institutional Responses: The Social Security System," in *The Subtle Revolution: Women at Work*, ed. Ralph E. Smith (Washington, D.C.: Urban Institute, 1979), pp. 239, 245.

2. Phillip Cutright, "Illegitimacy and Income Supplement," in *The Family, Poverty, and Welfare Programs*, U.S., Congress, Joint Economic Committee, 93rd Congress, first session (Washington, D.C.: Government Printing Office, 1973), p. 130.

3. Katharine Bradbury et al., "Public Assistance, Female Hardship, and Economic Well-Being," *Journal of Marriage and the Family* (1977), pp. 521, 533.

4. Nichole Questiaux and Jacques Fournier, "France," in *Family Policy: Government and Families in Fourteen Countries*, ed. Sheila B. Kamerman and Alfred J. Kahn (New York: Columbia University Press, 1978), p. 137.

5. Ruth Clark and Greg Martire, "Americans Still in a Family Way," *Public Opinion* (October/November 1979), p. 19.

6. James Cramer, "Births, Expected Family Size and Poverty," in *Five Thousand American Families: Patterns of Economic Progress*, 5 vols., ed. James N. Morgan et al. (Ann Arbor, Mich.: Survey Research Center of the University of Michigan, 1974–77), 2: 285–86.

7. Kristin A. Moore et al., *Teenage Motherhood: Social and Economic Consequences* (Washington, D.C.: Urban Institute, 1979), p. 10.

8. Sheila B. Kamerman, *Parenting in an Unresponsive Society: Managing Work and Family Life* (New York: Free Press, 1980), p. 33; Mary Jo Bane et al., "Child Care Settings in the United States," in *Child Care and Mediating Structures*, ed. Brigitte Berger and Sidney Callahan (Washington, D.C.: American Enterprise Institute, 1979), p. 20.

9. U.S., Congressional Budget Office, *Child Care and Preschool: Options for Federal Support* (Washington, D.C.: Government Printing Office, 1978), pp. 24–25.

10. Victor R. Fuchs, *Who Shall Live?: Health Economics and Social Choice* (New York: Basic Books, 1974), pp. 149–50.

11. U.S., Congressional Budget Office, *The Food Stamp Program: Income or Food Supplementation?* (Washington, D.C.: Government Printing Office, 1977), p. 24.

12. Heather L. Ross and Isabel V. Sawhill, *Time of Transition: The Growth of Families Headed by Women* (Washington, D.C.: Urban Institute, 1975), p. 122.

13. George Sternlieb and James W. Hughes, "The Uncertain Future of Rental Housing," in *America's Housing: Prospects and Problems*, ed. George Sternlieb et al. (New Brunswick, N.J.: Rutgers University Press, 1980), p. 264; Anthony M. Yezer,

Housing Problems of Families: Economic Issues (Washington, D.C.: National Research Forum on Families, 1980), p. 4.

14. George Sternlieb and James W. Hughes, "Some Economic Effects of Recent Migration Patterns on Central Cities," in Sternlieb et al., eds., *America's Housing*, p. 141.

15. Martin Rein et al., *The Impact of Family Change on Housing Careers* (Cambridge, Mass.: The Joint Center for Urban Studies of M.I.T. and Harvard University, 1980), pp. 4–37, 5–20.

CHAPTER NINE

1. National Commission on Employment and Unemployment Statistics, *Counting the Labor Force* (Washington, D.C.: Government Printing Office, 1979), p. 75.

2. Christopher Jencks et al., *Who Gets Ahead?: The Determinants of Economic Success in America* (New York: Basic Books, 1979), p. 81.

3. U.S., Department of Labor, *Continuous Longitudinal Manpower Survey* (January 1980, processed), report #10, tables 5–9.

4. Edward M. Gramlich, "Impact of Minimum Wages on Other Wages, Employment, and Family Incomes," *Brookings Papers on Economic Activity* 2(1976): 442–43; Sar A. Levitan and Richard S. Belous, *More than Subsistence: Minimum Wages for the Working Poor* (Baltimore, Md.: Johns Hopkins University Press, 1979), p. 155.

5. Sar A. Levitan and Richard S. Belous, *Shorter Hours, Shorter Weeks: Spreading the Work to Reduce Unemployment* (Baltimore, Md.: Johns Hopkins University Press, 1977), pp. 66, 68, 70.

6. Nancy S. Barrett, "Women in the Job Market: Unemployment and Work Schedules," in *The Subtle Revolution: Women at Work*, ed. Ralph E. Smith (Washington, D.C.: Urban Institute, 1979), p. 89.

7. Robert W. Bednarzik, "Worksharing in the U.S.: Its Prevalence and Duration," *Monthly Labor Review* (July 1980), p. 4.

8. David Robison, *Alternative Work Patterns: Changing Approaches to Work Scheduling* (Scarsdale, N.Y.: Work in America Institute, 1976), pp. 3, 31.

9. John D. Owen, "Workweeks and Leisure: An Analysis of Trends, 1948–1975," *Monthly Labor Review* (August 1976), p. 8.

10. Juanita M. Kreps, "Some Time Dimensions of Manpower Policy," in *Jobs for Americans*, ed. Eli Ginzberg (Englewood Cliffs, N.J.: Prentice-Hall, 1976), p. 186.

11. White House Conference on Families, *Listening to America's Families* (Washington, D.C.: Government Printing Office, 1980), p. 31.

12. Isabel V. Sawhill, talk before White Conference on Families, Baltimore, Md., 5 June 1980.

13. Nancy M. Gordon, "Institutional Responses: The Federal Income Tax System," in Smith, ed., *The Subtle Revolution*, p. 209.

14. *Congressional Record* (daily edition), 25 February 1980, p. E–807.

15. Michael C. Keeley, *Taxes, Transfers, and the Demand for Children: The Impact of Alternative Negative Income Tax Programs* (Menlo Park, Calif.: SRI International, 1979), p. 43.

16. Charlotte Saikowski, "Crisis and Comeback," *Christian Science Monitor*, 22 July 1980, p. 12.

17. Estimates based on data collected by the U.S. Department of Health and Human Services' Office of Domestic Violence.

18. Sanford J. Fox, *Juvenile Courts* (St. Paul, Minn.: West Publishing Co., 1977), p. 17.

19. Harry D. Krause, *Family Law* (St. Paul, Minn.: West Publishing Co., 1977), p. 40.

20. Thomas Grubisich, "Unwed Father's Custody Affirmed by Judge," *Washington Post*, 22 November 1980, p. B–1.

CHAPTER TEN

1. Tony Tanner, *Adultery in the Novel: Contract and Transgression* (Baltimore, Md.: Johns Hopkins Press, 1979), p. 97.

2. Albert Ellis, "Group Marriage: A Possible Alternative?" in *The Family in Search of a Future: Alternate Models for Moderns*, ed. Herbert A. Otto (New York: Appleton-Century-Crofts, 1970), p. 92.

3. Marjorie Honig and Nira Shamai, "Israel," in *Family Policy: Government and Families in Fourteen Countries*, ed. Sheila B. Kamerman and Alfred J. Kahn (New York: Columbia University Press, 1978), pp. 407–8.

4. Nena O'Neill and George O'Neill, *Open Marriage: A New Life Style for Couples* (New York: M. Evans & Co., 1972), p. 52.

5. Karl Marx and Friedrich Engels, *The Communist Manifesto* (Chicago: Henry Regnery, 1954), p. 31.

6. Karl Marx, *Capital: A Critique of Political Economy*, 3 vols. (London: George Allen & Unwin, 1949), 1: 469–71.

7. Friedrich Engels, *The Origin of the Family, Private Property and the State* (New York: International Publishers, 1969), pp. 58–59.

8. Harry D. Krause, *Family Law* (St. Paul, Minn.: West Publishing Co., 1977), p. 30.

9. David Mace and Vera Mace, *The Soviet Family* (Garden City, N.J.: Doubleday & Co., 1964), p. 221.

10. Zsuzsa Ferge, "Hungary," in Kamerman and Kahn, eds., *Family Policy*, pp. 72–73.

11. Alec Nove, *The Soviet Economic System* (London: George Allen & Unwin, 1977), pp. 11, 217.

12. Hedrick Smith, *The Russians* (New York: Ballantine Books, 1977), pp. 186–87.

13. Walter Lippmann, *A Preface to Morals* (New York: MacMillan Company, 1929), p. 88.

14. Charlotte Saikowski, "A Time for Families," *Christian Science Monitor*, 25 July 1980.

15. Deut. 24:12.

16. Mark 10:9–12.

17. Arthur W. Calhoun, *A Social History of the American Family: From Colonial Times to the Present*, 3 vols. (New York: Barnes & Noble, 1945), pp. 286–87.

18. Lawrence Stone, *The Family, Sex, and Marriage in England: 1500–1800* (New York: Harper & Row, 1977), pp. 41, 503.

19. Derek Bowskill, *All the Lonely People* (New York: Bobbs-Merrill Co., 1973), p. 146.

20. M. Scott Peck, *The Road Less Traveled* (New York: Simon & Schuster, 1978), p. 159.

INDEX

Abortion: in Eastern Europe, 44; and family size, 50; public opinion on, 152, 153; Supreme Court decision on, 39, 67, 152; of teenage pregnancies, 64

Age: of children in single-parent families, 62; at divorce, 12, 29; of female family heads, 113; and fertility rate, 43; at first marriage, 21–24; and poverty reduction by policies, 136; and remarriage, 34

Age distribution of American population, 44–46

Agrarian work roles, 82–83, 86, 123

Aid to Families with Dependent Children (AFDC), 144–48; for female-headed households, 115–16; and female labor force participation, 89; and teenage mothers, 153

Alimony, 174

Baby boom, post–World War II, 39, 41; and age at first marriage, 23

Bane, Mary Jo, 30

Beauvoir, Simone de, 117

Benefit-cost analysis of marriage, 24–27

Bernard, Jessie, 25–26, 179

Birth control. See Family planning

Birth rate. See Fertility rates

Black families. See Racial differential

Black female-headed families, 106–10

Broken homes. See Divorce; Female-headed households; Single-parent families

Business cycles and fertility rates, 49

Campbell, Arthur, 66

Carter administration, 4; family policy of, 124–25; and tax reform, 171; welfare reform under, 148

Child allowance. See Family allowance

Childbearing, and educational attainment of women, 39

Child care: benefits to children, 155; and female labor force participation, 81–82, 101–2; as female responsibility, 51–52; programs for, 153–55, 159

Child custody, 59, 62–63; law, 173–74

Child development: in broken homes, 69–72; and female labor force participation, 102

Childlessness, 8; and educational attainment of women, 51; in female-headed households, 146; and female labor force participation, 100; and fertility rate, 50–51

Child nutrition programs, 157

Children: abuse of, 172; in divorces, 13, 32, 57–64; in female-headed households, 72, 109; and marriage, time between, 41; number desired, 41, 50, 51; in poverty families, 134; premarital, 58, 64–67; and remarriage, 34; in single-parent families, 68–72; to unmarried couples, 35

Child support, 59–60, 68, 72–75; enforcement of, 74–75; in U.S.S.R., 184

Collective bargaining, maternity leave in, 167

Communes, 179–82

Communist family policy, 14, 182, 184–86

Comparative advantage theory of marriage, 25

Comprehensive Employment and Training Act (CETA), 163

Department of Health and Human Services, 75; Office of Domestic Violence, 172